AMERICA'S HORRIBLE HISTORIES

Are We There Yet?

Europeans Meet the Americans

by Elizabeth Levy

Illustrated by Mike Dietz

with Additional Material by J. R. Havlan

SCHOLASTIC INC.

New York   Toronto   London   Auckland   Sydney
Mexico City   New Delhi   Hong Kong

To Mara Jayne Miller, who was with me before
Columbus — E. L.

www.ElizabethLevy.com

Expert Reader: Richard W. Hill, Sr., (Tuscarora)
Haudenosaunee Resource Center, Tonawanda Seneca
Nation

Scholastic gratefully acknowledges the original inspiration of
Terry Deary's *Horrible Histories* series, published by
Scholastic Publications Ltd., London, U.K.

0-590-11831-5
Text copyright © 2001 by Elizabeth Levy

Printed in the U.S.A.
First Scholastic printing, September 2001

Contents

What's So Funny?

History is usually a random, messy affair . . .
Mark Twain, *A Horse's Tail*

The one who tells the stories rules the world.
Hopi saying

History and jokes can be horrible and wacky, often at the same time. The word "horrible" comes from the Latin word *horree,* which means to bristle, to make your hairs stand on end. "Wacky" comes from the Old English word *thwack,* from the sound a stick would make smacking something or someone. So at the very least, the horrible and wacky parts of history will wake you up.

There's a saying that if you don't know your own history, you are condemned to repeat it. I say that if we can't laugh at ourselves, we're in even worse trouble. There are facts and jokes in this book that will make you laugh out loud, some that will make you grin and groan, and others that will make you squirm.

It's a fact that Columbus thought he had gotten to India. That's why the Iroquois make fun of him calling them Indians. So while you're laughing at this and all the other jokes and cartoons in *Are We There Yet?*, remember the information in here is real, at least as far as anybody knows. But there is always new information being discovered and new ways of looking at history. Just remember, historians keep learning, and ideas about what really happened in the past sometimes change as quickly as most people change their underpants.

A joke from the Iroquois:

It's a good thing Columbus wasn't looking for Turkey, or they'd be calling us Turkeys.

The Search for History's Lost Jokes

North America never tried to hide. How could it? It's a huge continent stretching from the Arctic to Panama. Millions of people in North America built dazzling civilizations. They built giant pyramids along the Mississippi River as big as anything in Egypt. They sometimes lived in cities cleaner and more beautiful than any-place Europeans had ever seen. They had palaces with bathrooms when European kings were still peeing in fireplaces.

There's got to be a better way to do this.

Historians are pretty sure that for thousands of years, no one in Europe or Asia knew about these grand civilizations in North America. And the North Americans knew nothing about Europe or Asia. The story of when two *old* worlds collided — when the North Americans met the Europeans and vice versa — is one of the most famous and horrible stories in history. After Christopher Columbus sailed west from Spain in 1492, the history of North America and Europe changed forever. For most of the North Americans who were already here, it changed for the worse.

HOW TO BE A EUROPEAN EXPLORER

A - GET LOST AND GO INTO SOMEBODY ELSE'S HOUSE.

B - TELL THE PEOPLE WHO LIVE IN THE HOUSE YOU HAVE DISCOVERED IT.

C - TAKE ALL THE SPICES AND THE GOLD AND BRING THEM BACK HOME. AS AN EXTRA TREAT MAKE THE PEOPLE YOU FOUND DO ALL YOUR LAUNDRY.

D - GO HOME AND DEMAND TO BE NAMED THE GOVERNOR OF THE NEW NEIGHBORHOOD.

E - GIVE THE PLACE A NEW NAME, AND SAY THAT YOU NOW OWN IT.

The word "discover" comes from the French for "taking away the cover" (*dé*, away, and *couvrir*, cover). The European explorers didn't just claim to *discover* the continent of North America, they decided that if they plunked their flag on a place, they owned it.

The Name Game

The European explorers went around renaming everything they saw, including the women and men whom they met on their travels.

Most of the people living in North America simply called themselves "the people" in whichever of the continent's nearly 1,000 languages they spoke. They often had nasty names for all their neighboring enemies. Sometimes the Europeans mistakenly used those names.

The words "Native American" are sometimes used to replace Indian. Native means to be born in a place. If you took a rocket up to Mars and had a baby there, your baby would be a native Martian. Some descendants of the people who were here before Columbus say that "Indian" is not a name they would ever have called themselves, but neither is "American." "Let's just stick with Indian," they say, "rather than switch to Native American." So the name game can be confusing.

In this book, when it is known what a particular people called themselves, we use that name. If not, the people who were here first will be called the North Americans, since the Europeans in this book were not born in what would become known as America.

Elizabeth Levy

I've got a "name

game" for you: What's my name? Well, if you've already read the first two books of *America's Horrible Histories* (and I certainly hope you have!), then you know my name is Mel Roach. But like Shakespeare once said, "What's in a name? A roach by any other name would smell as stinky!" Or something like that. Anywhoo . . .

Get ready to read about a very exciting time in North America (that's the continent just north of South America). Millions of amazing people had lived here for a long time. They created magnificent civilizations and spoke

hundreds of different languages, though rarely at the same time (that would be really hard to understand!). These North Americans had

been here for thousands of years, until one day something weird happened. Their land was "discovered" by European explorers. "But how can that be?" thought the North Americans. "We've always been here. You can't say you discovered something if it's already been discovered by somebody else! These Europeans are cuckoo for Cocoa Puffs!" Well, the North Americans were half right. Those Europeans were cuckoo, but not for Cocoa Puffs. They were cuckoo for something else, and you're about to learn exactly what that was.

Chapter 1
Striking Vikings

Nobody Norse the Trouble I've Seen

Around the year 1000, the Vikings of Scandinavia didn't have a very nice reputation in Europe. Nonetheless, they *are* the first known people from Europe to visit North America. Actually, all the people in Scandinavia weren't Vikings. Mostly they called themselves the Norse people. Only the warriors and sailors who went on raids were called Vikings. The Vikings did commit some acts that would make you think twice about meeting one in a dark alley (and since the Vikings lived before electricity, all alleys were dark). Here is the story of the

TIME LINE

986
Bjarni Herjlfsoson, first known European to see America

1000
Leif Eriksson lands at Canada and calls it Vinland

1004
Vikings kill people they call Skraelings; Skraelings strike back

12

He claims *he's* named for his *red hair*, not the *blood* on his hands.

Vikings' first voyages to North America, according to *The Saga of the Greenlanders*, legends that the Scandinavians told and eventually wrote down.

I'm not worried about running into a Viking in a dark alley. I'm more worried about running into his hat.

Enter Erik the Red Eriksson

Erik the Red was kicked out of Norway because he murdered his neighbors after a minor argument. He was sent to Iceland, an island that Norway

1009
Leif's half sister, Freydis, helps set up colony in Vinland with 160 people

1016
Freydis murders her own people; Vikings go back to Greenland

2001
A Viking is still the mascot for Minnesota's football team

owned, which is about the size of Kentucky and is located in the cold sea northwest of England. In Iceland, Erik the Red killed more neighbors because they didn't return some wood beams that he lent them. After that, nobody wanted to be his neighbor. Erik was sentenced to three years as an outlaw, which meant anybody could kill him. Since one of the ways the Vikings punished people was to cut them open and make them walk around a tree as their intestines unwound, it wasn't surprising that Erik decided to get out of Iceland. He couldn't go back to Norway, so in 982 Erik headed west.

Give Erik credit. Sailing west with nothing but the stars to guide him was extremely diffi-

Fashion Statements of the Times: How to Dress Like a Viking Sailor

Drape yourself in a woolen blanket that goes down to your ankles and covers your head like a hood. Then sew two sheepskins together to make a sleeping bag — you'll need it. Every breaking wave and every raindrop is going to end up at the bottom of your boat, and you are sailing through the cold north Atlantic Ocean. Nobody will invent a way to pump water out of the bottom of boats until around Columbus's time.

cult. Viking boats moved by either using oars or one big sail. Sailing in shifting ocean winds was very tricky. On top of that, the boats often leaked. Although the Vikings were the best sailors of the Middle Ages, they mostly sailed close to land.

Erik stumbled across the largest island in the world, Greenland. It was so big that he didn't

know it was an island. Greenland is three times the size of Texas. It's a huge, barren island that has almost no trees; an icecap covers almost all of it. Still, Erik decided to call his find Greenland. He wanted others to join him and wisely realized nobody would come if he called it "very icy place with no trees." Some people from Norway were fooled and went to join Erik. One such family was the Herjlfsosons.

Bjarni Herjlfsoson Doesn't Get Off the Boat

In 986, Bjarni Herjlfsoson, just 20 years old, went to visit his parents in Greenland. He hit a bad storm. Blown off course, Herjlfsoson stumbled across a land covered with forests. It was probably Canada. Bjarni did not get off the boat. If he had, Canadians might be living in Herjlfsosonland. Nobody really knows why Bjarni didn't get off the boat and step on land. Some think he'd heard from his parents that Greenland didn't have any trees, so he knew that he was lost.

Leif Eriksson: Not Afraid to Get Off the Boat

When Bjarni finally got to Greenland, he found his parents. He told everybody he met

What's it going to take for me to put you in a boat today?

about the land *with* trees that was farther to the west. Among the people who heard his story was Leif Eriksson, Erik the Red's son. Leif bought Bjarni's boat.

In the summer of 1000 or maybe 1001, Leif sailed off to find the land that Bjarni had talked about. Leif got off the boat in what is now called Newfoundland, Canada. He called it Vinland, even though grapes don't grow that far north in Canada. Maybe Leif was a little leaf off the old family tree and decided to call it Vinland because he figured it would make people want to come.

In 1007, Leif's brother, Thorvald Eriksson, and 30 other Vikings decided to go live in

Vinland. When they landed, they set up some huts by the shore and spent the winter living on fish. In the spring, they went exploring. Thorvald and his men came upon three kayaks made out of animal skins. There was a man sleeping under each kayak. The Vikings killed two of the sleeping men, but one escaped. The names of Thorvald's victims have been lost to history. It is possible that these first North Americans to meet Europeans were the Beothuck of Newfoundland. They had been living there since around the year 200. The Beothuck covered their bodies, clothes, and weapons with a red paint made from a mineral oxide called ocher. Later, when the English

Early American Mosquito Repellent

Mosquitoes live in nearly every nation of the world, but the mosquitoes along the Atlantic coast of Maine and Canada can be up to two inches long. The Beothuck most likely rubbed their bodies with ocher as a form of mosquito repellent. Early North Americans also rubbed bear grease on their bodies to keep mosquitoes away, so just remember to keep a little grease handy if you're out in the woods.

met the Beothuck, they called them the "Red Indians." Historians think that might have been the origin of the term "redskin" for Indians.

The Vikings called the people they found in Vinland Skraelings, which means savage, wretch, or someone small or withered. In the saga of Thorvald they are described as "small and evil-looking, and their hair was coarse; they had large eyes and broad cheekbones." Some think the Skraelings should have called the Vikings "the enemies of good manners" for murdering them while they were sleeping.

Whoever the native Newfoundlanders were, they did not take kindly to strangers killing their kin. They attacked the Vikings. Thorvald got hit in the stomach with an arrow, and according to the sagas, as he was dying he said, "I notice I have put fat on my body. We have found a fruitful land, but we shall have little joy of it." Thorvald was so right.

A Girl Just Like Her Dear
Old Murdering Dad

Two years later, in 1009, the Vikings decided to try again. This time they sent three ships with

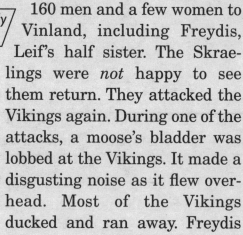

What a waste of a perfectly good moose bladder!

160 men and a few women to Vinland, including Freydis, Leif's half sister. The Skraelings were *not* happy to see them return. They attacked the Vikings again. During one of the attacks, a moose's bladder was lobbed at the Vikings. It made a disgusting noise as it flew overhead. Most of the Vikings ducked and ran away. Freydis picked up a sword from one of the slain Vikings. She screamed so loudly and fought so fiercely that the Vikings then rallied to hold their ground.

I'm actually a very nice girl, once you get to know me. Problem is, I kill people before they get to know me.

Like some other warriors in history, Freydis was not an easy person to be around in peacetime. She and her husband fought with other Vikings in the village. Her husband killed their male neighbors, but he hesitated to kill the women. Freydis took an ax and killed them herself. (Apparently she had more than an ax to grind.)

Remember Thorvald's last words? He turned out to be a good fortune-teller. The Vikings got little joy and little profit out of their discovery of America. After Freydis's murder party, the Vikings left Canada. They had only spent a few years there. They didn't find any of the wealth in the Americas. For centuries, they didn't even get credit in history books.

Fraud Alert: Even Yale Can Make a Mistake . . . or Did They?

In 1965, experts at Yale University said they had discovered a map of Vinland hidden in an old book. It looked real. Historians thought this map dated from around the year 1000. However, some scientific tests seem to prove that the map's ink wasn't invented until the

1920s. Furthermore, the map shows Greenland as an island, something geographers didn't know until the 17th century.

Historians are still arguing about whether the ink tests are accurate and whether the Vikings may have known that Greenland was an island. So the arguments about the famous "Vinland" map go on.

So How Does Anybody Know That the Vikings Really Got to America?

For a long time, many historians were not sure the Vikings *had* ever come to North America. The story of Bjarni, Leif, Freydis, and the others came from *The Saga of the Greenlanders,* ancient legends that were written down in the 13th century. But were the legends true? In 1964, archaeologist Anne Stine and her husband, Helge Ingstad, found real proof that the Vikings had actually come to Newfoundland, Canada. They found the proof in an area called L'Anse aux Meadows, the modern name for a place that for centuries was

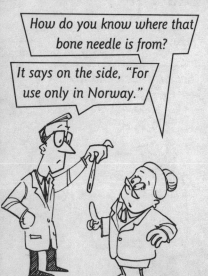

How do you know where that bone needle is from?

It says on the side, "For use only in Norway."

called Jellyfish Bay. Stine and Ingstad found needles and other tools made out of materials that were used only in Norway. Scientific dating of the needles shows that they and other remains date back to the year 1000, the same date given in Norse sagas for the voyages of the Eriksson family.

How historically important was the Vikings' discovery? Well, they did get to North America and they did write their story down, but they didn't stay very long. With the Vikings, the North Americans discovered that they needed to beware of strangers who came from the sea. After the Vikings left, for 500 years the people in the Americas got to go their own way without any interference from anybody else. So what were they doing for five centuries?

The Discovery Game #1

Historians have long wondered if perhaps other sailors besides the Vikings visited North America before Columbus. Here are a few of the main contenders.

458: The Chinese Discover the Pacific Coast of the Americas

Steeee-rike one!

A Chinese missionary, Huisan, wanted to spread the Buddhist faith. In 458, he sailed from China and was gone for 41 years. When Huisan returned, he told how he sailed for thousands of miles to "Fusang." Most historians think Fusang was Japan, but others think it was Mexico.

Fraud Alert: In 1980, the *Los Angeles Times* reported finding stones that looked like ancient Chinese anchors. It turned out that the stones *had* been carved by Chinese people, but by Chinese-Americans who came to California in the 19th century.

550: St. Brendan and the Irish Discover North America

St. Brendan was an Irish monk. He was already 70 years old (and not yet a saint) when he sailed west from Ireland in the year 550 because another monk had told him that the sweetest land lay to the west. St. Brendan was sure that this sweet land was the promised land. Brendan sailed west. Since North America is west of Ireland, some people think that St. Brendan sailed to either what is now Canada or the United States. In the 1970s, a group of explorers took off in an Irish curragh, or tarred leather boat. They wanted to recreate St. Brendan's voyage. They made it to Newfoundland, Canada.

Stories about St. Brendan say that he was attacked by insects the size of chickens. Some historians think that this is proof that the Irish monk landed in Newfoundland, a place famous for its ferocious mosquitoes. However, not one Irish artifact has been found from that time, so it's unlikely that St. Brendan really discovered America.

During the Middle Ages, the story of St. Brendan's voyage was as popular as stories about Superman or Batman are today. In one version, Brendan landed on the island and started to cook supper. When he built a fire, the island sank. The island was a whale.

Steeee-rike two!

The whale started to talk to him. Columbus knew about St. Brendan's legend, but as far as anybody knows, Columbus never ran into any talking whales.

1300: West Africans Discover America

Around 1300, one of the largest empires of the world was run from the fabulous city of Timbuktu, in what is now Mali in West Africa. The empire was perched right at the edge of the Atlantic Ocean. Around 1300, Timbuktu's emperor, Abubaker II, decided to find where the Atlantic Ocean ended. He outfitted 200 vessels and filled them with enough gold, water, and food for several years. Abubaker II ordered his sailors not to return until they reached the other side of the ocean or ran out of food. Some people are convinced that West Africans landed in Mexico, because the ancient Olmec sculptures there look African. The only problem is that the Olmecs lived there thousands of years before Abubaker is said to have sent his ships.

Steeee-rike three!

1405: Admiral Cheng Ho Discovers California

In the year 1405, Admiral Cheng Ho sailed out of China to explore new lands. He was given 317 ships and a crew of more than 27,000. Columbus's 60-foot vessels would have looked like dinky boats next to Cheng Ho's 400-foot ships. The admiral and his fleet sailed to what is now India, Sri Lanka, and the Persian Gulf, but there is no proof that they ever came to America. Still, Cheng Ho's ships were huge and *could* have sailed across the Pacific Ocean, so some historians speculate that he might have come to California or the northwest coast of Oregon. They are still looking for proof.

Let's just call that one a foul ball.

Boy, oh, boy, what

a family those Erikssons were, huh? I sure wouldn't want to get on their bad side. Didn't Papa Leif or sister Freydis ever hear of the saying "Love thy neighbor"? One thing's for sure, if I lived next door to those Erikssons and they ever came over to borrow a cup of sugar, I'd give them all the sugar I had!

But in all fairness, it does seem as if the Vikings were the first people in North

America (besides the North Americans, of course!). All those other people just sound like they were making their stories up. You can tell history is turning fishy when whales talk back.

But enough about all these people who claim they discovered America. Let's learn a little about the people we *know* discovered America . . . the ones who were here before the Vikings.

Chapter 2
North Americans on the Move

When historians try to guess how many people lived in North America between the years 1000 and 1492, their estimates depend a lot upon their viewpoint toward the people who lived here before Columbus. If North America was kind of an empty continent, then nobody had to feel too bad about the Europeans taking over. If it was full of people, then the Europeans had a lot to answer for, because after their arrival so many North Americans lost their lives either at the hands of newcomers or to the diseases they brought over.

TIME LINE

900–1100
Toltecs rule in
Mexico

960
Possible date of
founding of
Iroquois League

1100
Mesa Verde,
Colorado, at its
height; Mississippian
cultures flourish

1200–1300
Drought in
North America;
Delawares,
Apaches, Dinés,
and Mississippians
all on the move

30

Not long ago, many historians believed most of North America stood almost empty in 1492. They thought that maybe as few as 500,000 people lived in what is now the United States. They also thought that most of the people were not farmers but hunters and gatherers. Most of these historians had ancestors who had come to North America with the Europeans.

I don't see any people. Do you see any people?

Nope.

Recently, with the help of historians whose ancestors *were* here before 1492, many scholars have changed their minds. They now believe there were a lot more North Americans living here before 1492.

1325
Aztecs build Tenochtitlán

1400
Apaches and Dinés move south into Pueblo cultures

1428
Aztecs conquer as far south as Guatemala

1481
Period of unrest in Aztec empire begins

1486
Aztec emperor Ahuitzotl goes on a building and conquering spree

1998
Author moves into new apartment; roaches not far behind

The biggest population centers were in Mexico. Currently, the best guess is that more than 25 million people lived in Mexico alone. Maybe 10 million or 12 million lived in what is now the United States and Canada. These people spoke at least 500 to 1,000 different languages and lived very different lives from one another.

Counting Heads

If your teacher has trouble taking attendance, or if you have trouble guessing how many people are watching a Little League game, think how hard it is to count heads from before the days of written records. Here are a few of the tricks historians and archaeologists use.

- Most North Americans did at least *some* farming, mostly of corn. By studying ancient planting fields, archaeologists can make pretty accurate guesses about how many people lived near the fields.

- Studying ancient burial grounds also gives hints about populations.

Is there anybody counting roach motels? That's a good way to get a roach count.

- The Aztecs in Mexico kept written records and took pretty accurate head counts, especially about all their enemies. Historians use these records to figure out the population of Mexico from 1350 to 1500.

Despite the huge mountain ranges that made travel difficult, North America was criss-crossed with trading routes. Not only did people trade with one another, but they moved into each other's territories. With so many different languages and cultures, people rubbed up against strangers all the time. Sometimes they got along, but lots of times they rubbed each other the wrong way, and they ended up at war.

The People of the Longhouse Get a Peace Plan That Works

The Haudenosaunee of what is now New York State and other states of the northeast were made up of many nations, among them the Huron, Mohawk, Seneca, Onondaga, Cayuga, and Oneida. The Haudenosaunee, or People of the Longhouse, were always fighting with the Algonquin, and they had horrible wars among themselves. Eventually, these nations became known collectively as the Iroquois; that's what the French called them. The Haudenosaunee never would have called themselves Iroquois, because they knew it meant "terrible people" in the language of their enemies, the Algonquin.

The oral tradition of the Haudenosaunee says a Peacemaker set out to bring an end to the warfare among the neighboring tribes. The Haudenosaunee do not use the Peacemaker's actual name out of respect because they believe he was born to bring peace to the Earth.

After many years, the Peacemaker had reached a total of 50 tribal leaders and convinced them to join in a league of peace. The Seneca, Cayuga, Onondaga, Oneida, and Mohawk nations united under America's first unwritten democratic constitution, called the Great Law of Peace. After the Europeans came to America, the Haudenosaunee became known as the Iroquois League or the Iroquois Confederacy. It was the most important political unit north of Mexico, and it fascinated some later colonists, who considered the League one of their models for the United States Constitution.

This gives me a great idea!

THE IROQUOIS LEAGUE

Here is just a snapshot of some of the other things that were going on during the roughly 500 years between the arrival of the Vikings and that of Columbus.

Human Hearts, the Toltecs, Quetzalcoatl, and Butterflies

From about 900 to 1100, the Toltecs ruled what is now Mexico. Like the cities of the Maya and other ancient civilizations in Mexico, Toltec cities had huge pyramids that reached toward the sky. At the top of the pyramids, archaeologists believe, humans were sacrificed. Now, we have no witnesses of sacrifices, only the art and books of the Toltecs that show people being sacrificed. Was the art documentary or fanciful? Archaeologists and historians are not sure. The Toltecs surrounded their temples with gigantic sculptures of warriors. This has led many historians to believe they were a warlike people, and their art has none of the playfulness of Maya art and other art from ancient Mexican civilizations.

The Toltecs wrote their legends down. Most historians think that the Toltec legends, like the sagas of the Eriksson family, were based on real people. According to these legends, in the year 986, a young king, Topilitzin, tried to stop the practice of human sacrifice. He preached that the feathered serpent god, Quetzalcoatl, didn't want any more human hearts but wanted snakes and butterflies instead.

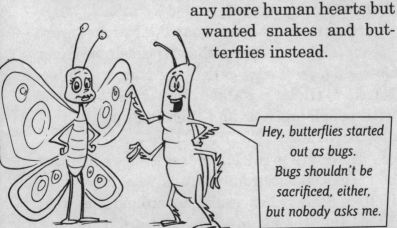

Hey, butterflies started out as bugs. Bugs shouldn't be sacrificed, either, but nobody asks me.

Topilitzin had enemies who drove him into exile. Some historians of ancient America think it is possible that followers of Topilitzin, calling themselves Toltecas, or Toltec travelers, moved north along the Mississippi River.

Toltec Traces

So did the Toltecs really ever come north from Mexico and settle in what is now the United States? Nobody is sure; archaeologists are still trying to figure it out. No actual Toltec artifacts have ever been found to prove this theory. However, the Natchez people of what is now southern Mississippi and Louisiana have legends of rulers they call Great Suns. The Great Suns were thought to have come from what might have been Toltec territory. Some historians believe that the Natchez legends are evidence that they were originally ruled by Toltecs.

Historians do know that the Natchez were great traders. Along the Mississippi River there is a trail now called the Natchez Trace. Natchez traders walked this trail to trade with people upriver and then float goods back downstream.

There are many other traces of what might be ancient Mexican influence in what is now the United States. For example, around the year 1000, the Hohokum people of what is now

Natchez Trace Parkway More than 410 miles of the original Natchez trail between Natchez, Mississippi, and Nashville, Tennessee, have been preserved as a parkway. Along the way you can see many ancient mounds. In **Spiro, Oklahoma, Etowah, Georgia, Moundville, Alabama,** and the **Cahokia Mound State Historical Site** in **Illinois** you can see the remains of the centers of Mississippian culture. There is also **Toltec Mounds State Park** in **Arkansas.** Despite its name, most archaeologists do not believe it was built by the Toltecs, but it does have one of the largest mounds in the United States. What happened to the Mound Builders is still one of the great mysteries of North America.

Phoenix, Arizona, built huge ball courts very similar to those found in Mexico.

　　Also by the year 1000, there were hundreds — probably thousands — of towns with large mound-like pyramids up and down the Mississippi River and its tributaries. These pyramids were built in the same style as those found in Mexico. Archaeologists call these towns and their inhabitants the Mississippian cultures. The Mississippian cultures extended over what is now

Speaking of Mexican influence, I sure could go for a few crumbs of a taco right now.

almost all of the southeastern and central parts of the United States. Even after the Mississippian cultures had declined, many ancient Americans traced their roots back to those great city-states.

Musical Chairs: Ancient Americans Change Places and Dance

Around the year 1300, America became cooler and drier. Growing corn and farming became much harder. So did hunting, because the great buffalo herds suffered from the drought. Everyone moved to try to find a better place to live. If you had looked at a map back then, it would have seemed as if the people were playing musical chairs in what is now the United States.

- The people who were once called Apaches and Navajos pushed south from western Canada. Eventually, they reached the Southwest, the

Nearly every state has sites that have preserved some of the North American way of life from the time between the Vikings and Columbus. Here are just a few that deal with the period between 1000 and 1492. **Mesa Verde, Colorado,** is a huge outdoor museum that has been declared a World Heritage Site. **Sioux Indian Museum** in Rapid City, South Dakota, **Monument Valley Navajo Tribal Park** on the Utah/Arizona border, **Tantaquidegeon Lodge Museum and Foxboro Museum** and the **Mashantucket Pequot Musuem** in Foxwood, Connecticut, feature replica villages you can walk through. The **Pocono Indian Museum** in Bushkill, Pennsylvania, is dedicated to the life of the Leni-Lenape.

land of the people who had built Chaco Canyon and Mesa Verde. (Navajo means "enemies of plowed fields." That's what the people of Chaco Canyon and Mesa Verde called their new neighbors. The Navajo now call themselves Diné, which means "people" in their own language.)

• The Leni-Lenapi people began a great migration that took them from west to east. They are sometimes called the Delaware but much prefer their own name, Leni-Lenape, which means "true people."

• The Algonquin people who lived near the Great Lakes spread out toward the Atlantic coast. Sandwiched in between the Algonquin were the Haudenosaunee, or People of the Longhouse, whom the French later named the Iroquois.

Aztecs on the Move

Around 1300, the same drought that caused so many North Americans to migrate also caused the people who would become the Aztecs of Mexico to pull up stakes. The Aztecs believed that they came from a place up north called Aztlan, which means "land of white herons." Some scholars are investigating whether the

Be careful with these things, they're all made from gold.

AZTEC MOVERS

May I Take Your Order?

Chocolate, tomatoes, and tortillas are all foods that are still available today. But the following are some other Aztec specialties that you probably won't find on a menu anytime soon.

- Thistles and rats with sauce
- Newts
- Water fly eggs
- Tadpoles
- Salamander larvae
- Lake scum (The Spaniards claimed this was as tasty as Spanish cheese.)

Aztecs might have come from Nevada or Utah. They are studying the Aztec language, Nahuatl, and comparing it to the languages of the Lakota, Dakota, and other North Americans who lived in what is now the western part of the United States. Nahuatl is still spoken by 1.2 million Mexican Indians. Chocolate, tomato, tamale, and chili are all Nahuatl words.

According to their legends, after leaving Aztlan, the Aztecs wandered around for years, searching for a home. Their legends fore-

I never knew so many of my favorite words were Nahuatl. I've been speaking it all my life.

told that they would finally find one wherever they saw a cactus growing out of a rock with an eagle on it.

The Aztecs wandered into the fertile Valley of Mexico where the Toltecs had once ruled. The Aztecs' hummingbird god, Huitzilopochtli, gave them the name "Mexica," thus the origin of the name Mexico.

Good Morning!

Huitzilopochtli was the Aztec god in charge of the sun's journey across the sky. To help the sun rise every day, Huitzilopochtli had to chase his sister, the moon, out of the sky. It was a hard job: Apparently the only way to do it was to drink blood, known as "most precious water." The Aztecs believed that their gods needed blood so that the sun would rise every day and the rain would fall for the crops.

The Culhuacans, who already inhabited the Valley of Mexico, and their allies promptly attacked the Aztecs. The Aztecs were way outnumbered. They were pushed into swampy lands in the middle of a lake, more than a mile above sea level. There, according to their legends,

The Mexican flag has an eagle on it.

they saw a cactus and an eagle on an island and shouted something like, "Honey, we're home!" The Aztecs started building islands with mud from the lake. They called their island home Tenochtitlán, and this island city would became one of the wonders of the ancient world. The site is now Mexico City.

The Army That Traveled on Its Stomach (and Turned a Few, Too)

Fighting was one thing the Aztecs were very good at. They quickly went from the "people whose face nobody knows" (what their neighbors called them because the Aztecs moved around so much) to the "in-your-face people." The Aztecs developed the most disciplined and fearsome army in all of North America. At times, they had more than 100,000 warriors. The Aztec army, like armies everywhere, traveled on its stomach. One reason for their success was that they were incredibly well organized in supplying their forces with food — mostly tortillas — wherever they went.

For the Aztecs, there was no activity more glorious than war. It was considered lucky to die on the battlefield. After an heroic death, a person was promised a new life as a beautiful butterfly or hummingbird. According to the Aztecs, there were three glorious ways to die:

1. in a battle
2. playing the ball game
3. giving birth to a child

What about being stepped on? How come nobody thinks that's a glorious way to die?

Those conquered by the Aztecs were forced to pay tribute. The Aztecs kept very detailed records. Each year the capital city of Tenochtitlán received 7,000 tons of corn, 4,000 tons of beans and grains, and two million cotton cloaks. They also got precious jewels, gold, and silver and humans to use as sacrifices for their gods. The great-

SACRIFICE THIS WAY

The sun will come out tomorrow.

Fashion Statement of the Times: How to Dress Like an Aztec Warrior

Since war was so glorious, naturally you needed a gorgeous outfit. The elite Aztec warriors wore suits made of jaguar skins or eagle feathers. Even foot soldiers wore quilted cotton tunics that the Spaniards eventually adopted. Aztec warriors carried round wooden shields covered with animal hides; many were beautifully decorated with feathers. These shields are collectors' items today. High-ranking Aztec officers wore towering headdresses of reeds, and feathers on their shoulders. This headgear was supposed to frighten their enemies and let their own warriors know where their officers were. Unfortunately, when the Aztecs fought the Spaniards, it was easy for the Spaniards to pick off their leaders.

Let me guess. You're the leader, right?

est glory for a warrior was to capture his enemies alive so they could be sacrificed later.

Not Just Great Warriors, Great Artists, Too (and Very Clean)

With all that tribute flowing in, the Aztec capital city of Tenochtitlán grew more beautiful and even larger. It became bigger than any city in Europe at the time, with a population of between 100,000 and 300,000 people.

Give or take a few. I love the way historians make guesses about ancient numbers.

The streets of Tenochtitlán were washed daily. The houses were said to be spotless. When the Europeans saw the city and its inhabitants, they were amazed that nobody was begging on the street and even more awed by how clean everything and everybody was. Europeans rarely took baths. In Europe, most people didn't use bathrooms because there weren't any. You did your business in a pot in your bedroom and then threw the slop out onto the street. Meanwhile, the Aztecs had separate rooms for their toilets and nearly every home had a steam bath.

This is a real step up from what you're used to in Europe, eh?

An Emperor with Real Dedication

The Aztec emperor, Ahuitzotl, who ruled from 1486 to 1502, was a great warrior. He went on the attack, bringing almost all of central Mexico under Aztec command. He finished the Great Temple of Tenochtitlán, which had been

Everybody into the Aztec Sauna!

1. Go to the fire room and light a fire. This will make the walls of the steam room next door get red-hot.
2. Go in the steam room. Splash water on the walls until the room fills with steam.
3. Sit and relax. If you're bored, watch your pores open or watch your buddy's pores open.
4. Get a servant or a friend to rub you down with twigs or grass.

When you meet the Europeans, they won't believe how clean you are.

under construction for many years. For the Great Temple's dedication, Ahuitzotl was said to have sacrificed 20,000 people. Some historians argue that the Spaniards made up that number to make the Aztecs look bad; still, nobody doubts that a whole lot of sacrificing was going on.

Naturally, the neighbors of the Aztecs were getting mighty sick of watching their best young people die on Aztec altars. Many of the Aztecs' neighbors, such as those in nearby Tlaxcala, began to long for someone, *anyone,* to help them get rid of the hated Aztecs. Unfortunately for them, their wish was about to come true.

From 1000 to 1492, there were waves of North Americans crisscrossing the continent. In the summer of 1492, 90 Europeans, mostly from Spain, came to North America on a different kind of wave. Led by an Italian, Christopher Columbus, they came by ship across the Atlantic Ocean. They didn't know about the Aztecs, but they sure wanted to get their hands on some gold.

The Best–Worst Sacrifice List

Best: If you were a particularly cute male captive, you were worshiped as a god for a year and taught how to dance and play the flute. You were given four beautiful maidens. On the last day of your life, you mounted the steps of the temple, smashing one by one the clay flutes that you had played during your time of glory. Then you were sacrificed on an altar, but, hey, you'd had a great year.

If you'll excuse me, I think I'll go practice dancing and playing my flute some more.

Next Best: The most common sacrifice was to be given a ritual bath and then stretched over a sacrificial stone where a priest would cut out your heart.

Not So Good: Having your head cut off — usually reserved for female victims dressed as goddesses.

Still Not So Good: Being tied to a scaffold and shot with darts or arrows.

Most Unfair: Your leg is tied to a stake. You're given a war club without blades. Your opponent is given a club with razor blades. Surprise, surprise! Your opponent wins. You get cheers if you put up a good fight.

Yuckiest: You're thrown in a fire and taken out while still alive and then thrown back until nicely roasted. Finally, your heart is cut out.

The Discovery Game #2

When the Europeans eventually reached the great cities of the Aztecs and saw the huge mounds and pyramids that existed throughout North America, they couldn't believe that the North Americans had built those monuments and created that artwork themselves. Stories arose about how another civilization from another continent — or even another planet — got to North America long before Columbus.

Around 1500 B.C.E.: Egyptians Discover America

The Olmecs, the first great civilization in North America, lived at the same time as the Egyptian pharaohs. Egypt is in North Africa. Many people think the great stone heads the Olmecs carved look African. In 1969, adventurer Thor Heyerdahl sailed a boat made out of papyrus reeds

I guess I better get to work on Ra II.

from Egypt to America. His first boat, the *Ra*, sank. *Ra II* made it, but that doesn't prove the ancient Egyptians did.

Around 1000 to 500 B.C.E.:
The Phoenicians Discovered America

The Phoenicians wore purple, invented the alphabet, and were the best ancient sailors on the Mediterranean Sea, but did they come to America? In 1874, the Reverend

M. Gass of Davenport, Iowa, claimed he found a stone with Phoenician writing on it. "Eureka!" he shouted. (Or something like that.)

Fraud Alert: The stone had some letters that weren't even invented when the Phoenicians were around. The Reverend Gass later admitted that he had carved the stone himself as a hoax.

It sure was easy to see through Gass's theory.

600 B.C.E.: The Hebrews Reach the Americas

The Book of Mormon tells of Hebrew people who came to ancient America from Palestine. According to the Book of Mormon they were led by a prophet who sailed across the ocean to the Americas around 600 B.C.E.

Did you say geeks or Greeks?

347 B.C.E.: The Greeks Discover America

Plato is one of the most famous philosophers of all time. He was a teacher in ancient Greece in 347 B.C.E. Like all good teachers, he loved to tell stories. Plato talked about a fabled lost continent that sank beneath the sea in the western ocean. He called this continent Atlantis. Many Europeans claimed North America was the lost continent of Atlantis. Another Greek myth claimed that the Amazons, a tribe of fierce women warriors, lived on an island. The Spanish linked this Greek myth to the people they found in North America.

55 B.C.E.: Romans and Druids and Celts — Oh, My!

In his salad days, Julius Caesar had a lot of trouble with a warrior tribe called the Celts who lived in what is now Great Britain. The Romans decreed that every Celtic priest or Druid be put to death, but legend has it that some Druids escaped. After English colonists settled in New England they found some caves in the hills that were very much like the Druids' caves back home in Great Britain. But caves look pretty much the same all over the world. Did the Druids come to America? There isn't really any proof.

Around 1100: The Legend of the Seven Cities of Gold

According to Spanish legend, sometime around 1100, seven bishops escaped Moorish rule and fled from Spain by crossing the "Sea of Darkness," as the Atlantic Ocean was called in those days. They landed at a place they called Antilla. Antilla had rivers of golden sand. The bishops built cities of gold. (Think of golden sand castles.) Later, Spanish explorers would search all of North America for those seven cities, which they called Cibola.

Another Popular Theory: Aliens Discovered America

Some people believe the pyramids along the Mississippi and in Mexico as well as other earth sculptures found in North and South America are landing sites for alien spaceships. Some people would believe anything rather than accept that ancient Americans could develop high civilizations on their own.

Nobody's ever *going to believe this!*

Whew! It must

have been tough working for the Census Bureau anytime between 1000 and 1492. Imagine trying to get an accurate count of how many people lived in North America back then. I mean, how would you even get anybody to understand the questions: Do you have indoor plumbing? Do you own your own pyramid? You'd have to speak between 500 and 1,000 languages. I'd probably just take a wild guess about the number of folks and tell my boss "lots." Sound good to you?

In the meantime, while you're trying to count heads, all these other people are claiming *they're* the folks who made North America great. I mean, Druids? Come on! That sounds like something your mom makes you drink when you have a fever.

"Be sure to drink plenty of Druids, honey."

I have to admit, though, it's kind of cool to think maybe aliens from outer space landed in America. Maybe, just maybe, when ET phoned home, he was actually just calling Cleveland.

Well, I'm sure the next people to reach the continent seemed like aliens to the North Americans already there.

Chapter 3

Oy, Columbus!

Columbus was born in Genoa, Italy, in 1451. He probably first went to sea when he was 9 or 10. By his teens, Columbus had learned to steer, set up sail, weigh anchor, and judge distances at sea by eye. He became so skilled as a sailor that later even most of his enemies had to admit that he was as keen a navigator as had ever lived.

Columbus was obsessed with the idea that the best way to quickly reach India, China, and Japan was by sailing west. This flew in the face of what everybody else said, but Columbus didn't care. He took his scheme to the king of Portugal and the king of England, who both turned him down. Columbus decided to go to Spain and put his case

TIME LINE

1492
Columbus lands in the Caribbean in October; Guacanagari, an Arawak chief, rescues Columbus in December

1493
Columbus returns to Spain, gets big parade; Arawaks kill the crew that Columbus left behind

1495
Columbus begins a slave trade

before King Ferdinand and Queen Isabella.

One of the royal advisers said something like, "Hey, wait a minute. Chances are this guy will sail off and be dead within a month, but if he does get to India or China, what do we have to lose? We can get bankers to front the money, and we've got this little town, Palos, by the sea. They owe us. Make them give this Columbus guy a few ships." Columbus got his royal backing.

Columbus's Cruise

Columbus collected scissors, knives, coins, beads, needles, pins, mirrors, and little bells that hunters hung on hawks' necks. Columbus planned on trading these trinkets for all the gold he expected to find on his voyage. These gifts have puzzled historians for a long time. If Columbus planned to reach the Indies, did he

1495–1500
Arawaks die from European diseases; Arawaks rebel but are squashed

1503
Black slaves from Africa brought in to replace Arawaks

1506
Columbus dead at age 55

2001
On October 12, there are Columbus Day sales instead of "sails"

Whatever Christopher Wants, Christopher Gets

Here is what Christopher Columbus told King Ferdinand and Queen Isabella he wanted:

• Make me a noble. I want everyone to call me "Don Christopher."

• Make me "Admiral of the Ocean Sea."

• I want to be viceroy of everything I discover. (*Roy* means king. *Viceroy* was the title for someone who was a little like a vice president to a king. A viceroy ruled a colony by the authority of a king or queen.)

• I want 10 percent of the gross of all transatlantic trade.

Columbus got it all!

No wonder the king and queen turned him down at first. Even big-time movie stars don't get 10 percent of the gross!

I sure hope the rulers of India and China need a bunch of scissors, knives, coins, beads, needles, pins, mirrors, and little hawks' bells.

really think the rulers of India and China would be impressed by this stuff? Maybe the bells, scissors, and so forth were all that Columbus could afford. After all, the queen and her bankers weren't really anxious to invest a huge amount of money in something they were sure would fail. Columbus was only given three small ships, the *Niña*, the *Pinta,* and the *Santa María*.

Most of the 90 members of Columbus's crew were professional sailors. On these early European voyages to North America, the sailors did all the work. There were no soldiers on any of Columbus's three ships. His crew was armed with just a few crossbows and harquebuses, heavy guns that often exploded in your face when fired.

Give me all your gold or I'll shoot myself in the face.

More Fashion Statements of the Times: How to Dress Like a European Sailor

- Put on a tunic, which is like a dress that ends a little above your knees.
- Put on tight stockings. Hope you have good legs. Having good legs was much more important to men than to women, and people often gossiped about men's legs. You might want to wear different-colored stockings, which was the fashion.
- Put on a red velvet cap. Columbus wore a red velvet cap, and so did many of his men. Those velvet caps turned out to be something that every West Indian cacique, or chief, wanted. You can never account for fashion.
- Rub in a lot of dirt. Nobody took a bath or washed his clothes the whole voyage.
- You might want to bring nose plugs because your clothes stink, but real sailors didn't mind the stench.

The *Niña*, the *Pinta*, and the *Santa María* tried to sail as close to one another as they could. The Atlantic Ocean is huge, and for safety's sake sailors at sea want to stay together. There was a lot of shouting back and forth, and the captains would even visit the other ships. Some historians like to talk about how miserable the journey was. It was certainly filthy. Ships were filled with lice, rats, and roaches. Sailors took cats aboard to kill rats.

On board, the men drank beer and cider

because they didn't trust fresh water, which got slimy and full of bugs. Meals consisted of an occasional warm stew of pickled beef and pork and moldy biscuits. Eating the biscuits was a bit

They don't know what they're missing. Maggots are the best part!

time-consuming because you had to pick the maggots out of the biscuits first. There were no sleeping quarters. Sailors simply had to bunk down wherever they could find a dry spot — and there weren't many dry spots on board the ships.

Columbus and his crew hit perfect sailing weather for the first two weeks; in one day they sailed 174 miles. On the night of October 11, 1492, Columbus thought he saw firelight from land flickering near the horizon. He told his men to drop anchor.

Guanahani, October 1492

Picture a lush Caribbean island: white beaches, green palm trees full of coconuts, tall pine trees, and grasses. This was the land that Columbus had spotted. Its people called the place Guanahani. They spoke a language called Arawak. *Hurricane, hammock,* and *barbecue* are

Thank you, Arawaks! Barbecue is the most beautiful word in any language— except for chocolate.

all Arawak words. The fire Columbus spotted possibly came from a barbecue.

The Arawak cacique, or chief, had a group of nobles and priests around him called Taino. Because Columbus dealt mostly with the elite or Taino, Taino is sometimes what the people of these Caribbean islands are called in history books.

After the ships dropped anchor at dawn, the Arawaks must have watched from the trees as Columbus and some of his men rowed to the beach in a little rowboat. Columbus waded ashore, knelt, and prayed. He planted a flag with a green cross and the letters F and Y on it, F for Ferdinand and Y for Ysabelle (which is the Spanish spelling of Isabella).

Eventually, the Arawaks came out of the woods to meet Columbus. The Arawaks and the Spaniards started trading immediately.

Columbus was struck by the beauty of Guanahani and the kindness of the island's people. The Arawaks offered Columbus parrots, cotton, carved wood, and most important, food and water. They invited him to feasts where they sang songs and recited their legends. The Spaniards gave the Arawaks glass beads and hawks' bells.

Gee, thanks. Just what I've always wanted.

On the day of his very first encounter with a North American, Columbus wrote to the king and queen of Spain, "These people are very simple . . . they will make excellent servants. Should your majesties command it, all the inhabitants could be taken away . . . or made slaves on the island." Nobody has recorded what the Arawaks thought, but does anybody really believe that they were thinking, "This guy's lost. We're not anywhere near India, but maybe if we're lucky they'll make slaves out of us"?

Why *were* the Arawaks so nice to Columbus? Columbus wrote that the Arawaks, both women and men, thought the Spaniards were gods. There is no real proof that this is true. The Arawaks belonged to a culture where being generous showed that you had immense power. Only someone powerful could afford to give anything away. So it is likely that the Arawaks were hoping to impress Columbus by giving him gifts and that they did not think that he was a god.

Columbus was disappointed with the small amount of gold that he found. Then he saw a ring in one Arawak's nose. Columbus got very excited

and pointed to it. The Arawaks got the idea that Columbus and his men really, really, *really* wanted gold. They began a game that would be played out over and over whenever the North Americans met Europeans, "Oh, you want gold? It's not here. Why don't you go to . . ." This was a way of getting rid of the Europeans by sending them on a wild goose chase.

Columbus only spent a couple of days on Guanahani. Then he sailed off, taking a number of Arawaks with him on the ship. Some historians believe these Arawaks were forced to go. Others think that

I guess the Arawaks were never told that you should never accept a ride on a stranger's rat-infested ship.

perhaps on this first encounter, the Arawaks agreed to go. Humans often opt for adventure.

For months, Columbus went from island to island in the Caribbean, constantly searching for gold, and constantly being told it was just around the corner on the *next* island.

> Pssst. *Have you heard the rumors about these new guys sailing around here? They're trying to trade glass for gold. They're lazy and refuse to get any of their own food. And worst of all, they can't tell a good joke.*

On December 5, 1492, Columbus saw the mountains of Bohio. Bohio in Arawak means the "source of all good things." Today, it is the island shared by Haiti and the Dominican Republic. It is one of the largest islands in the Caribbean, and in 1492, Bohio probably had a population of at least three million Arawaks. To Columbus, everything about the island was like Spain, and so he named it "Little Spain," or Hispaniola.

> *Why don't cannibals eat class clowns? Because they taste funny.*

At first, Columbus couldn't help noticing that nobody came down to greet his ships. The Arawaks on board warned Columbus that the islanders on Bohio "ate people." To Columbus, the name they were saying sounded like "cannibals," and he coined the term.

Columbus sent an armed party inland and found a village of 1,000 houses and more than 3,000 people. The Bohio villagers fled, but Columbus's guides chased them, shouting not to be afraid, that "the Christians are from the sky and they give lots of beautiful things to anyone they meet." Once again, this is Columbus's report of what his guides tried to say. For all he knew, they were saying, "Run for your lives. These Christian explorers have hairy faces and only want gold." As far as we know, Columbus never learned the Arawak language; instead he relied on his Arawak guides to learn Spanish.

Spanish 101

The teacher smells funny and has a hairy face.

Whatever Columbus's guides said, it seemed to work. The inhabitants of the large town came by the thousands to greet the Spaniards. They brought parrots to the ship to trade for European goods. Columbus and his crew probably got sick of parrots, but the Arawaks considered parrots a great gift.

Columbus heard tales of a great ruler on Hispaniola called Guacanagari, the most important cacique in the northeast part of Hispaniola. By now, thousands of Arawaks were coming to Columbus's ship, day and night. Canoes were at the side of the ship 24 hours a day.

Shipwreck!

On Christmas Eve 1492, after four exhausting days with thousands of visitors, Columbus set sail along the coast of Hispaniola, wanting to find Guacanagari's village. Columbus hadn't slept in two nights. At 11 o'clock at night, he finally went to bed. The water was calm.

That's because it was the night before Christmas, and not a sea creature was stirring.

The sailor who usually steered the *Santa María* also decided to go to sleep. He handed the tiller to a young boy, despite orders that this was never to be done. The boy ran the ship onto a sandbar. When the boy heard a grinding sound, he yelled. Columbus woke up and ordered his crew to drop anchor and to try to back up the ship, but the planks on the bottom of the ship broke and water rushed in. Some sailors escaped

The Blame Game
Who caused the shipwreck of the Santa María?
a) Columbus. He was the admiral,
so he should have taken responsibility. But NO!
b) The sailor in charge of the tiller.
He should never have given it to a boy. But NO!
c) The boy. He shouldn't have fallen asleep. But NO!
d) Blame somebody who wasn't even there.

(answer: d) In his logbooks, Columbus blamed Guacanagarí, saying it was all his fault because Columbus had been trying to get to his village.

to the *Niña;* the other sailors stayed aboard the *Santa María*, still trying to save her. Columbus sent word to Guacanagari, begging for help.

Even though he had never met Columbus (though clearly he had heard of him from other Arawaks), Guacanagari is said to have wept at the news of Columbus's sad plight. He immediately sent many people in large canoes to help unload all the goods and sailors from the *Santa María*. The Arawaks did an incredible job. Although the *Santa María* broke apart, not one life was lost, and all the goods on board were saved. Columbus wrote to the king and queen of Spain that "in no part of Spain could everything have been placed in such good security without losing a lace-point."

When Columbus and his crew were safely on shore, Guacanagari treated Columbus to a feast. He gave Columbus a big mask with gold eyes and ears, plus other gold jewelry that Guacanagari himself put on Columbus's head and neck. Columbus took off a necklace of very nice beads of many pretty colors and put it on Guacanagari. He also took off his cape, the one he had worn that day, and put it around Guacanagari's shoulders. Columbus sent for some colored boots and put them on Guacanagari's feet and gave Guacanagari a large silver ring.

With one ship wrecked and the *Pinta* having sailed off on its own to Cuba, Columbus didn't

Boy! We look great!

have enough room to take all his men back to Spain. He decided to leave 39 sailors behind. They built a town out of the timber from the shipwrecked *Santa María*. Columbus called the town Navidad, because it was founded on Christmas.

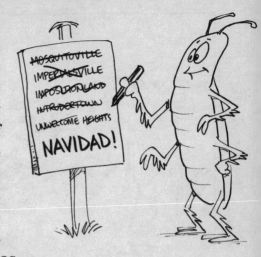

On January 4, 1493, Columbus took six captured Arawaks, many parrots, and what gold he could find, along with the other plants and objects he had collected, and sailed back to Spain on the *Niña*. They had very bad weather sailing back, perhaps even running into a hurricane. Columbus, his crew, and the six Arawaks had a very hard time of it. They eventually ran into the lost *Pinta*.

After a rough two-month voyage, Columbus landed in Spain on March 15, 1493. Columbus marched into Barcelona, cheered by crowds all along the way. The six Arawaks followed him, carrying parrots. His crew carried the gold and the rest of the strange treasures that Columbus had collected.

Good Things About Being the Admiral of the Ocean Sea:
1) All the glory
2) Riches
3) Don't have to carry anything

A Bad Day at the Beach

Meanwhile, the 39 Spaniards on Hispaniola were having a lousy day at the beach. Part of the problem was that they didn't want to do any of the work of farming or gathering food themselves. Guacanagari had promised Columbus he would help the men. Apparently, even Guacanagari couldn't or wouldn't do anything when the Spaniards robbed a neighboring tribe and kidnapped their women. The tribe counterattacked and slaughtered every last one of the

Royal Godparents

The king and queen of Spain and their son, Prince John, acted as godparents to the six Arawaks who came to Barcelona with Columbus. The Arawaks were baptized as Christians in a ceremony in that city's great cathedral.

I hope they got good presents.

Spaniards. If you look at things from the Bohios' point of view, 1493 was a very good year. They had killed off all the Spaniards who had been robbing them, and they must have thought Columbus would never come back.

Little did they know, Columbus *was* coming back. In 1493, he returned with about 1,200 people, including many nobles, soldiers, and six priests. Seventeen ships sailed from Spain, carrying not just men and supplies but this time sheep, pigs, horses, and a pack of attack dogs. The trip from Spain took less than a month. Soon, the Spaniards would go back and forth pretty easily, even without frequent-sailing mileage.

Columbus had promised the king and queen that when he got back to Navidad, he'd send shiploads of the gold that he was sure his men had collected. Instead, Columbus found all his men dead, many lying on the ground, their corpses rotting.

Good Gift for Spain

Bad Gift for Spain

The End of the Arawaks: The End of Columbus

The second voyage marked the beginning of the end for the Arawak people. Columbus ordered his men to set up a new trading post on land that was marshy and full of mosquitoes. The Spaniards got sick and nearly starved because they refused to try to grow any crops themselves and often would not eat the Arawak food.

But the illness of the Spaniards was nothing compared to what happened to the Arawaks. Within months, they were dying from smallpox, measles, and other European diseases from which they had no immunity. Even the Spaniards were shocked by the speed with which the Arawaks were dying.

Columbus knew that his glorious enterprise was crumbling around him. He couldn't find gold. He had to send the king and queen something. So, in February 1495, he rounded up 1,500 Arawaks as slaves. He hoped the slaves would make up for the lack of gold. There was only room for 500 slaves on the ships, so he told the Spanish settlers to help themselves to the rest. From then on, Columbus would think of slaves as his only form of gold. On the return journey to Spain, 200 of the slaves died and were thrown into the sea.

Meanwhile, the Spanish settlers on Hispaniola soon ran through all their supplies. Few of the Spaniards were farmers, and they had expected to simply pick up gold from the North Americans. When Columbus returned as governor he began "giving" a certain number of Arawaks to each Spaniard in a

I bet the native peoples of Mexico, Florida, Texas, Arizona, New Mexico, and California weren't too happy about that!

European Diseases in America: Why Did They Kill So Many?

Diseases like smallpox, plague, measles, typhus, and scarlet fever first ripped through the Arawaks and then other North American communities time and again. It happened whenever native North Americans met Europeans. Europeans also caught diseases they had never had when they first met native Americans, but the North Americans had it much harder.

Why was this so? Historians and doctors and other scientists are still studying the history of germs and trying to figure it out. Here are a few of the things they've come up with:

• Europeans had been living with animals like horses, cows, and pigs for thousands of years, but when those animals came to America, they brought diseases that native Americans couldn't fight off.

• In Europe at the time, usually only the very young or very old still died from illnesses like smallpox and measles. When a disease swept through North America, both adults and children got sick. Soon there was nobody who could take care of the sick or dying. And there was nobody left to plant the fields. This was a pattern that would repeat itself again and again.

system called the *encomienda*. The king of Spain made it official in 1503. The Spaniards would later take this system, which was really a form of slavery, with them to Mexico, Florida, Texas, Arizona, New Mexico, and California.

Gold Fever That Kills

The Spaniards' thirst for gold was unquenchable. Columbus demanded that each Arawak bring him a hawk's bell filled with gold every three months. A hawk's bell is pretty tiny, about the size of a thimble. However, there wasn't enough gold for even this small amount. If the Arawaks did not bring in enough gold, sometimes the Spaniards would cut off their hands or arms and let them bleed to death. This is, of course, not a good idea if you want someone to bring you more gold.

The Arawaks tried to save themselves. There were at least 12 slave rebellions. Several caciques tried to fight the Spaniards to protect their people. Oddly enough, it wasn't the guns that gave the Spaniards the advantage so much as their horses and dogs. Spanish guns were not that good and often exploded in a soldier's face, but the Arawaks had never seen horses before, nor dogs as vicious as Spanish hunting dogs. Even today, a handful of mounted police officers and officers with dogs can control a large group of people.

Many of the Arawaks who survived the rebellions died from overwork or starvation, others from diseases brought over by the Spaniards. Still others committed suicide. Mothers even killed their own children to prevent them from being killed by the Spaniards. In 1498, Columbus's brother did a head count of the Arawaks living on just half of Hispaniola. He came up with a figure of 1.1 million. By 1535, less than 50 years later, there were only 500 Arawaks left. By as early as 1503 or 1505, when Columbus was still alive, the Spaniards on Hispaniola and the other islands began to bring in African slaves to work the fields that the dying Arawaks were leaving empty. There are conflicting stories about what happened to Guacanagari, the chief who saved Columbus's life. Some have him fleeing into the mountains and dying a wanderer, others say that the Spaniards burned him at the stake.

Columbus: Admiral of the Mosquitoes

Columbus was a disaster as governor of Hispaniola. Whether criminals or nobles, most of the Spaniards who tried to settle the lands controlled by Columbus came to hate him. Some Spaniards now called him "admiral of the mosquitoes." He certainly found more mosquitoes than he did gold. They complained again and again to King Ferdinand and Queen Isabella that Columbus was a terrible leader. The king and queen sent someone to find out what was going on. This man decided the settlers were right, and he sent Columbus back to Spain in chains. The king and queen of Spain pardoned him and removed the chains. They let him make two more voyages. But Columbus, believing that God was punishing him for being vain, refused to wear his admiral's uniform and instead put on a monk's robe.

Columbus died on May 20, 1506, when he was 55 years old. He had remained convinced that he had found islands off India. One of the last things Columbus wrote was, "They all made fun of my plan then; now even tailors wish to discover."

It's a good thing

Columbus was such a great sailor, because he didn't seem to be much good at anything else. First of all, he thought America was India. That's silly! All you need to do is look at a map of the world and you'll see that not only is North America a completely different shape from India, but it's also usually in a completely different color! No wonder those Arawaks

gave Columbus parrots instead of the gold he wanted. The Arawaks were a lot smarter than Columbus thought they were!

Maybe if Columbus had just set up a shop and hung out a sign, "We Buy Gold," the Arawaks would have brought him all kinds of gold! But Columbus just wanted to take the islanders' gold without giving them anything for it. That's not fair! If you ask me, Columbus wasn't the Admiral of the Ocean Sea, he was the Chicken of the Sea. But I guess anybody who has a holiday named after him can't be all bad — especially if we get to take that day off from school!

Well, maybe the next people to explore the not-so-new new world will be a little nicer . . . or will they?

Chapter 4

Name-a-Continent Contest

King Ferdinand and Queen Isabella of Spain wanted to be sure that none of the other European royal families would try to horn in on Columbus's discoveries. After all, it was Spaniards who had put up the money for his trips. In 1493, the king and queen asked Pope Alexander VI to declare that all the new lands belonged to Spain. However, King John II of Portugal insisted that Portugal should have its share because they had been sending out explorers even before Spain.

TIME LINE

1494
Pope Alexander VI divides the world between Spain and Portugal

1497
John Cabot sails to Canada for the king of England

1498
John Cabot sails off again and is lost at sea

1499
Amerigo Vespucci makes his first voyage to America, sailing for Spain

82

In 1494, Pope Alexander VI had Spain and Portugal sign the Treaty of Tordesillas. The pope declared that there was a north/south line through the world that ran through in the middle of the Atlantic Ocean. Any "undiscovered" lands west of the line would go to Spain. Any lands east of the line would go to Portugal. Since Brazil juts out east of that imaginary line, Brazilians still speak Portuguese.

My little brother and I divided our bedroom the same way.

In 1494, there were probably anywhere from 90 million to 112 million people already living in what would be called North and South America. They neither knew about nor cared about the pope, Spain, Portugal, or any silly treaty. However, in Europe, other countries cared, and they were not happy being left out. Among the most unhappy was King Henry VII of England.

John Cabot: Mystery Man

In 1492, England was still recovering from the Hundred Years' War with France, which had ended in 1453. Being an island, England was a seafaring country, but it had lost out in the pay-for-an-explorer contest when the English King Henry VII had turned down Columbus. Now King Henry was kicking himself.

The Tudor monarchs were an independent lot. (King Henry's son Henry VIII would have six wives and start a new religion. His granddaughter, Queen Elizabeth I, was just as feisty.) King Henry VII wasn't going to let a little thing like a papal decree, which declared that all the newly discovered lands belonged to either Spain or Portugal, stop him. He wanted a piece of the action for England.

In January 1497, John Cabot offered to sail for England. Nobody knows much about him. There aren't any portraits, letters, or even a scrap of handwriting. The name John Cabot sounds so sturdily English, but one of the few facts known about Cabot is that he was definitely Italian, most likely from Genoa, the same town as Columbus. His name was probably originally Caboto. It's even possible that Cabot was born in the same year as Columbus and Queen Isabella. He was definitely in Spain when Columbus came back in triumph from his first journey. Then Cabot moved to England, had a family, and lived in Bristol. Above the town was Brendon Hill, named for St. Brendan, who was supposed to have visited there nearly 900 years before.

Hey! Can I help blow out the candles, too?

Cabot convinced the king of England to let him make a journey west like Columbus. He promised to try to find a seagoing passage to India. And his plan wasn't going to cost the king a penny. John Cabot would raise the money himself. Cabot could only get money for one ship. The ship's name was *Mathew* and it was little, only 50 or 60 feet long, or just under the size of Columbus's smallest ship, the *Niña*.

In May 1497, John Cabot left Bristol. Only 18 men sailed with him. After 33 days of sailing, on June 24, 1497, Cabot and his crew saw land. It was the coast of Canada, very close to where the Vikings had landed. There were no people around, but Cabot saw signs that people lived there, such as fishnets and sticks used to weave nets. Eventually, Cabot went ashore with King Henry's banner, plunked it into the ground, and left a cross. He declared that the land belonged to England.

Apparently, John Cabot didn't walk on shore again. As navigators go, he rates an A+ for sailing but a D– for exploring. Some histori-

REPORT CARD
JOHN CABOT - - - - - - - - -
SAILING . . . . A+
EXPLORING . . . . D–
GYM C

Revenge of the Lady Mosquitoes

If Cabot fled back to England because of the mosquitoes, it might not have been the first time that these American insects had driven out Europeans. Remember those mosquitoes as big as chickens that attacked St. Brendan?

The rocky coast of Newfoundland, Canada, is full of small dips that catch rainfall and melting snow. It's a great place to look for tadpoles, but it's an even better breeding place for swarms of mosquitoes. A single female mosquito can lay up to 400 eggs at once. If you ever get a mosquito bite, it was a lady who did the biting. Only females can puncture human skin.

ans think it was the mosquitoes that turned Cabot and his crew away.

Cabot sailed back to England in just 15 days. He arrived home on August 6, 1497, and went to see the king. He had no gold, no people, no parrots, but still Henry VII was pleased. The king gave "10 pounds to hym that founde the new Isle." And that's how Newfoundland, Canada, got its name: New Found Land. Once Europeans think something is new, they tend to keep calling it "new." For example, they named New York in 1664, and that's been its name ever since, even though it isn't very new. Then there's New England, New Spain, New Amsterdam, and New Mexico.

In July 1498, Cabot tried to find a passageway to India again. This time five ships went with him. They never made it. One ship ran into trouble in Ireland and turned around; John Cabot was never heard from again. He must have died at sea. Nobody knows what happened to him.

After Cabot's voyage, English fishing boats began to regularly fish the waters off the Atlantic coast of what is now Canada and New England. The many codfish amazed the English. English fishing ships traded with North Americans such as the Beothuck, Abeneki, and Pasamaquoddy of Maine. English metal tools and kettles became prized possessions among these tribal groups, but soon people along the Atlantic Coast began falling ill from mysterious diseases. This was long before any English came to live in North America.

Amerigo Vespucci, Great Storyteller

The Hopi people have a saying that is quoted in every one of *America's Horrible Histories*: The one who tells the stories rules the world.

Sounds good to me!

STORY TELLING
CONTEST
TODAY!

1ST PRIZE:
GET YOUR
NAME ON
A MAP!

Amerigo Vespucci may not have been the first European to reach America, but he was a great one for telling stories. So maybe he deserves the prize of getting his name on the map.

Amerigo Vespucci was a wealthy man from Florence, Italy. His last name means wasp. Vespucci was richer than Columbus and had a better education. His father owned a spectacular library and collected books and manuscripts. Apparently, even as a young boy, Amerigo loved maps, which were beautifully hand-drawn in those days.

Vespucci moved to Spain in 1492. He became friends, or at least acquaintances, with Columbus and helped raise money for Columbus's second and third voyages. Then Vespucci decided he wanted to see these new lands for himself. In 1499, he sailed to South America. He was the first European to see the mouth of the Amazon

River in what is now Brazil. Because of the pope's treaty, Vespucci realized that he had landed in Portuguese territory. He offered his services to the King of Portugal. He made another trip, now sailing under the Portuguese flag. In January 1501, Vespucci found the beach of a huge bay and river. He called it Rio de Janeiro, which means River of January. The Brazilian city of the same name is still famous for its beautiful beaches.

Read It Here! Naked Women! Naked Men! Cannibals!

Vespucci happened to be a great writer. Some historians think he made up a lot of his stories. Amerigo was always running into naked women and cannibals. Unlike Columbus, who seemed reluctant to give up the idea that he had found India or China, Vespucci suspected early on that they had reached an entirely new continent. He was the first European to declare that he had found a *Mundus novus* — a "New World." Vespucci wrote, "In those southern parts, I have found a continent more densely peopled and abounding in animals than our Europe or Asia or Africa. [They] go around entirely naked and not only offer to their king the heads of their enemies whom they have killed, but also feed eagerly on the flesh of their conquered foes." Cannibalism and naked men and women were popular images of the New World. They helped to sell books written by the explorers.

How to Get Your Name on a Map

A German printer and mapmaker named Martin Waldseemüller loved Amerigo's letters about the New World. In 1507, he made a huge world map, using information from the voyages of Columbus, Cabot, and Vespucci. Waldeseemüller put the name "America" on the new continent, because he liked the way it sounded. It sounded like a continent, like Africa or Asia. Six years later, however, Waldeseemüller made a new map. This time, he didn't think it was a good idea to call the new land America. He realized it should probably be called Columbia, after Columbus. He left the word America off, but it was too late. The name America stuck.

I have to admit,

I always wondered where the name America came from. I mean, I've heard of Captain America; I've even heard of Miss America; but I had never heard of Amerigo Vespucci. He sounds like he's named after a motorized bike! You know, Vespas, those little motor scooters that zip through traffic like wasps.

I'm still not sure what made any of these Europeans think they had a right to name the New World after themselves or claim it for some king or queen who already had more than their fair share of . . . every-thing! Those explorers got here way after the Aztecs and the Arawaks and the Haudenosaunee. But I can tell you this: It's a good thing that guy Waldseemüller didn't name the New World after himself. I wouldn't even be able to pronounce the name of my own continent!

Anyway, I'm starting to get the idea that no matter what the explorers' names were, the North Americans didn't really want them around. The explorers talked funny, they smelled funny, and they grabbed everything they could get their hands on. Even I wouldn't want to have anything to do with them — and I'm a cockroach!

I wonder if the next newcomers to the new world will be any better. Something tells me . . .

Chapter 5

The Spaniards on the Move

After the death of Columbus, many Spaniards, including King Ferdinand, began to have doubts about whether the islands Columbus had found were worth keeping. Not much gold was coming in, and the king was having to spend more time than he wanted to listening to different conquistadores argue about who was doing what to whom. Some Catholic priests worried whether it was right to kill or make slaves of everyone they saw.

TIME LINE

1513
Balboa wades into Pacific Ocean, claims all lands touching it belong to Spain; Ponce de León gives Florida its name; the Calusa drive Ponce de León out of Florida

1515
Las Casas converted to antislavery cause

1516
All conquistadores required to tell "Indians" to submit to the Roman Catholic Church

94

The Requirement: Not Something to Put on Your College Application

In Spain, a great debate began about whether or not the "Indios" were really human. The king and his court declared that because they *did* have souls, the "Indios" should be given a chance to be saved by converting to Catholicism. Every Spanish conquistador had to carry a copy of *le Requerimiento,* or the Requirement. When the conquistador came across a native, he was supposed to read out loud that the pope and the king of Spain greeted the natives "with love." If they would accept the Roman Catholic Church and submit to Spain, they would be treated kindly. If not, the conquistador was told to read the words, "I will take your wives and children and make slaves of them and will sell them as such, and will take all your goods and do you all the mischief I can. . . ."

The conquistadors were supposed to give the natives time to think about it. The Requirement became a joke. Spanish warriors would read it to the trees or to dead bodies after they had killed

1519
Balboa gets beheaded as a traitor by the Spaniards

1521
Ponce de León returns to Florida and gets killed by a poisoned arrow; Spaniards leave Florida alone for seven years

2001
MTV televises spring break from Florida; some Floridians wish college students would leave them alone for seven years, too

Bartolemé Las Casas: A Spanish Priest Caught Being Good

In 1502, Bartolemé Las Casas, a Spanish Catholic priest, came to Hispaniola. He promptly began acquiring Arawak slaves. In 1515, while reading the Bible, Las Casas decided his own soul and the souls of all the Spaniards were in danger because of their brutality toward the Arawaks. He spent the rest of his life writing and pleading that the people that the Spanish called the "Indios" be treated well. Las Casas was one of the few Spaniards to write about the daily life of the Arawaks. He noticed that Arawak men and women treated one another more as equals than women and men did in Spain.

everyone. Or they'd read it while people were asleep, and the words "do you all the mischief I can" became famous because there were plenty of mischief makers from Spain who were ready for an adventure.

Ponce de León Hits Florida

The name Juan Ponce de León means John of the Lion's Paunch. He was just 19 when he sailed with Columbus on his second voyage. Ponce de León was famous for his red hair, his bravery, and his vicious dog, Berezillo, who also had a reddish coat. Ponce de León trained

Berezillo to catch Arawaks by the throat and kill them. He used to brag that Berezillo knew good Arawaks from hostile ones just by the way they smelled. Ponce de León was so proud of his dog's ability to tear hostile Arawaks limb from limb that he gave his dog the pay, allowance, and share of booty assigned to a soldier.

Ponce de León was made captain of all the soldiers on an island called Borinquén, which we

A guy could grow old looking for something like that.

now call Puerto Rico. There wasn't much gold in Puerto Rico. In 1513, Ponce de León heard rumors that there was a fountain of youth somewhere north of Puerto Rico. Anyone who drank the waters from this natural spring would be made young again. Ponce de León wasn't sure whether to believe the rumors, but he figured maybe he'd find gold.

On April 3, 1513, Ponce de León and his men sailed north from Puerto Rico. They spotted land, probably around what we now call Daytona Beach, just a few days after Easter. The Spaniards call Easter *Pascua Florida,* or the "Feast of Flowers," and that's how Florida got its name.

Ponce de León jumped onto the beach and claimed the land for Spain. He read the Requirement on empty sands. The area wasn't really empty, though. It was the territory of powerful warriors who called themselves the Calusa. They lived in towns and cities with temple mounds built on huge bases of seashells. The Calusa had large canoes that they lashed together. They traded with the people of Puerto Rico and Cuba. They had heard about the Spaniards

Fashion Statement of the Times: How to Dress for Invading Florida

- Don't forget your helmet! Even the poorest soldiers wore steel helmets. The most popular helmets had ends that curved up, making you look like you were wearing a little sailboat. Helmets weighed about six pounds each.

- Wear a chest plate. Sometimes this was made of welded pieces of steel, but that's very heavy. Most of the time you'd wear a tunic made out of chain mail, or small metal rings linked together. Be careful: Even though chain mail is lighter than steel, an arrow can pierce a chain mail chest plate. The leaders would also have leg armor to protect them on horseback. No Spanish conquistador would travel without his armor, which weighed about 60 pounds.

and knew enough not to want them on their land.

The Calusa sent out an ambassador in a canoe; he spoke Spanish, having probably learned it on one of the islands. The ambassador told the Spaniards that their ruler would "deal" with them tomorrow. The next day, the Calusa attacked in a long line of canoes. They paddled their canoes as fast as they could toward the anchor chains of the Spanish ships. They tried to cut the chains so that the ships would float back out to sea. The Spaniards fought them off.

Several of Ponce de León's men were killed. Others were wounded. The Spaniards sailed off. Everywhere in Florida the Spaniards tried to anchor their ships, the Calusa showered them with arrows. Ponce de León gave in to his men's demands that they go back to Puerto Rico. When the Calusa saw the Spaniards sail off, they may have thought they had gotten rid of them forever.

Eight years later, in 1521, Ponce de León tried again. He got to Florida in February and hit one of those cold spells that today drive tourists nuts. The Spaniards had brought no warm clothing with them. Without warning, the Calusa people attacked. By now they had learned that they couldn't fight the Spaniards at close quarters. They kept retreating, drawing the Spaniards deeper into the woods. Ponce de León got hit by an arrow with a poisonous tip. His men got him back to the ship, and they sailed away from Florida. Ponce de León died from the poison in

Historical Museum of Southern Florida, Miami, Florida Many of the exhibits here show how the Calusa people lived.

Hey! This isn't what the travel agent led us to expect!

June 1521. The Calusa people of Florida had kept the Spaniards off the mainland of what is now the United States for at least a little while longer.

Balboa Takes a Swim in the Pacific

Like Ponce de León, Vasco Núñez de Balboa had been a soldier in Spain who was out of work. He was an excellent swordsman, apparently fun-loving, full of zip, and liked women. He also had a way of getting in and out of trouble.

Balboa came to Hispaniola in 1501 when it was still governed by Columbus. Balboa tried farming pigs, but like most Spanish nobles, he was a lousy farmer. The only thing he seemed to like on Hispaniola was his huge, yellow-colored dog, one of the puppies of Ponce de León's dog. He named the dog Leoncico after Ponce de León.

Boy, are they going to be surprised when they see us!

Balboa soon got into so much debt that he was in danger of going to jail. He decided to stow away on a boat headed for Panama. He took nothing except the clothes on his back, his sword, and Leoncico. He and the dog hid in an empty flour cask. When they got out to sea, he jumped out and said, "I'm here."

The captain wanted him killed, but some of the men spoke up for him, saying something like, "Hey, he's a great guy with a sword, and we might need him." When they got to Panama, the men voted to put Balboa in charge of things there. The captain sailed back to Spain and immediately started spreading stories at court about what a good-for-nothing, disloyal subject Balboa was.

Meanwhile, Balboa started exploring the area to the north of Panama. Although weighed down by heavy armor, Balboa and about half of his men made the journey through a tropical jungle, across the Serranía del Darién. On September 27, 1513, Balboa was the first European to see the Pacific Ocean. He tasted the water to make sure it was salty. With Leoncico at his side, he waded in. He lifted his shield and said, "I now take possession in fact of law of these southern seas, lands, coast, harbors, and islands with all territories, kingdoms, and provinces which belong to them or may be acquired in whatever manner, or whatever reason by whatever title, ancient or modern, past present or future, without let or hindrance. . . ."

Now, the people who already lived in Panama, much less Mexico, California, Oregon, Peru, and so on, all of whose land touched the Pacific Ocean, did not think they belonged to Spain. It's hard to figure out how an ocean can "belong" to anyone. But never underestimate the arrogance of those European explorers.

Balboa spent two months lolling about on the beach and collecting gold. Meanwhile, a new governor came from Spain. At first, the new governor and Balboa got along, but once again, the popular Balboa clashed with the governor. Someone poisoned his dog, Leoncico. Balboa was  put on trial for mistreating the people of Panama, for betraying the trust of the king, and for leading a revolt. He was found guilty and on January 21, 1519, Balboa was beheaded.

Ouch! That's gotta hurt!

Sometimes it seems

like the only thing meaner than the explorers
themselves were the explorers' dogs. I guess
they didn't have obedience school back then.
Ponce de León's dog even got paid to be mean.
Can you imagine that? A dog getting paid?
What does a dog do with money? One time
I saw a dog wearing a sweater, so maybe they
spend it on clothes. I even saw a dog wearing little boots once, so I guess maybe

they spend it on shoes. I wonder if a dog who buys footwear gets mad at himself for chewing up his own shoes. Either way, I think it's a waste of money to pay a dog.

But enough about those mongrels, let's get back to the explorers. To be honest, I'm starting to give up on the idea of any of them being nice. Now I'm just starting to worry about how long it will take before the North Americans finally meet their match!

Chapter 6

The Aztec Army Meets Its Match

The Spaniards wanted gold. Just 500 miles southwest as the crow flies from where Columbus first landed, there was more gold and silver and wealth than any Spaniard had ever laid eyes on. It all belonged to the Aztecs, and they didn't have any intention of letting it go.

In This Corner: Moctezuma II

In 1502, Moctezuma II became emperor of the Aztecs. He was apparently as much a worrier

TIME LINE

1502
Moctezuma II named absolute monarch of Aztecs

1519, February 10
Hernán Cortés sails for Mexico

1519, November 8
Cortés and his Tlaxcalan allies enter capital city of Tenochtitlán

1520
Moctezuma II killed and Spaniards driven out of Tenochtitlán

106

as a warrior, a man who often couldn't sleep at night. He was very interested in religion, not just his own but other religions as well. He also wrote poetry and loved songs and jokes.

If he couldn't sleep, the emperor didn't have to worry about being bored. There were about 100 apartments in his palace. They were decorated with red-and-green marble and jade, colored tapestries, and beautiful carved wood. The palace was full of hidden courtyards with beautiful ornamental fountains and rare

1521, April
Tlaxcalans and Cortés lay siege to Tenochtitlán

1521, August
Fall of Tenochtitlán

2001
"Moctezuma's revenge" is the name still given to a stomach bug that sometimes hits tourists in Mexico

How to Live Like an Emperor

- Be carried almost everywhere, lounging on a litter.

- When you do step down, have nobles sweep the ground in front of you and cover the ground with beautiful cloth so your feet never touch the earth. Don't worry if your foot does touch ground, though — the bottoms of your sandals are made of gold.

- Be offered a hundred dishes at mealtime. Don't worry about your table manners because you eat behind a gold screen.

- Don't let anyone look at your face or turn his or her back on you. Even your brothers and sisters should walk out of the room backward.

- If you get bored or are interested in what the common people are thinking, sneak around the city and ask people what's going on. (That's what Moctezuma did.)

Sounds nice. I wonder what he paid in rent.

flowers. Within the palace walls there were zoos filled with rare animals.

Moctezuma II had a lot on his mind. It wasn't an easy time to be an Aztec emperor. Many of the Aztecs' enemies, such as the Tlaxcalans, were sick of paying tribute. And it was the year One Reed, the year that Quetzalcoatl had vowed to return and destroy everything. Year One Reed was the European year 1519.

In This Corner, Hernán Cortés

By 1519, various Spanish ships had begun to explore the coastline of Mexico. They reported that they had met people who were warlike but had a lot of gold and silver. Hernán Cortés lobbied hard with Governor Velázquez of Cuba to get the job to explore this area. Cortés signed up 533 soldiers, but only 13 of them had guns. His army had only 16 horses and 14 cannons. Just as Cortés was about to sail off, Velázquez changed his mind about putting him in charge. So Cortés snuck out at night with 11 small ships. Velázquez swore revenge on Cortés, but Cortés didn't care.

He was sure he would find gold and silver. Cortés and his men sailed to the mouth of the Tabasco River near present-day Veracruz, Mexico.

The Tabasco River? Sounds hot!

As the conquistadores went to the shore in rowboats, they were met by thousands of Tabascan warriors, their faces blackened with war paint. The Tabascans were Aztec allies. Cortés and the conquistadores waded through a hailstorm of arrows. The fighting continued for three days. The Tabascans had never fought against steel swords or guns or men on horses before; still they kept attacking. However, they were used to wars where you didn't try to kill your enemy but capture them. The Spaniards fought to kill. By the end, as many as 800 Tabascans lay dead on the battlefield. Although many Spaniards were wounded, only two of them had died.

Malinche: Traitor or Heroine?

The Tabascans sent ambassadors to negotiate a truce. As was their tradition, the ambassadors brought gifts, among them a woman slave named Malinche, whom Cortés renamed Doña Marina. She was the daughter of a chief in the Aztec realm, and she had been sold into slavery in the Yucatán. Malinche knew Nahuatl, the Aztec lan-

María de Estrada, Conquistadora

There were at least three women on board Cortés's fleet. They cooked or acted as companions. At least one of them, María de Estrada, became a famous warrior herself.

There are only a few mentions of de Estrada in the histories of the conquest of Mexico, but they are tantalizing footnotes. Some historians believe that María de Estrada was a converted Jew who had escaped the Inquisition in Spain. She was said to be an expert horsewoman and fierce with both lance and sword. De Estrada survived the conquest of what came to be known as Mexico; she lived there until 1548.

guage, and also spoke Mayan. Soon she learned Spanish. She became Cortés's most trusted adviser and later had a son with him.

I'd say those ambassadors were about three days too late.

Malinche told Cortés about the legends of Quetzalcoatl and that the Aztecs were expecting him back in the very year that Cortés had landed. With Malinche's help, Cortés came to realize the Aztecs had many enemies and that he could play a game of divide and conquer.

Nothing happened in Moctezuma's empire without his knowing about it. He sent ambassadors to Cortés, telling him to stop marching into Aztec territory. Unfortunately, his ambassadors, as was tradition, also brought gifts, including a beautiful gold disk that represented the sun. Cortés told Moctezuma's ambassadors that the Spaniards suffered from a fever that only gold could cure.

Personally, I'd rather have a fever that only cookies and ice cream could cure.

The Enemy of My Enemy Is My Friend

Cortés and his army moved inland and soon got to the land of the Tlaxcalans. Although the Tlaxcalans hated the Aztecs, at first they considered Cortés just another invader. They attacked Cortés's army and almost destroyed him then and there. For three weeks the battle raged. Cortés tried to bury the 45 soldiers who had died so the Tlaxcalans wouldn't realize they were winning. Cortés was weakened by fever. Most of his soldiers were wounded. Cortés retreated and began raiding nearby towns, killing women and children. Through Malinche he sent messages to the Tlaxcalans, seeking peace.

I hate to say it, but don't invite greedy people to dinner, especially my relatives.

With Malinche working with him, Cortés convinced the Tlaxcalans that he would be able to free them from the Aztecs. The Tlaxcalans agreed to join their army with Cortés's to fight the Aztecs.

Moctezuma Makes a Mistake

Moctezuma knew that Cortés had joined forces with the Tlaxcalans, but he couldn't seem to decide what to do. At first, he sent ambassadors with more gifts to Cortés. Unfortunately, the gifts were more gold. Naturally, that only whetted Cortés's appetite to see the capital city of Tenochtitlán for himself. Finally, for some reason, Moctezuma changed his mind and invited Cortés to come visit.

On November 8, 1519, Cortés and the Spanish entered Tenochtitlán with of tens of thousands of Tlaxcalans marching behind them. Moctezuma, carried on a golden litter, greeted him, wearing a brilliant green feather robe decorated with jewels. He wore golden sandals, and even the soles of his shoes were gold.

I can't think of any other shoes that go with a green feather robe.

Cortés and Moctezuma exchanged formal greetings. Cortés took off a necklace of pearls and placed it around Moctezuma's neck. Moctezuma

Personally, I like my shrimp fried, but to each his own.

told a servant to give Cortés two necklaces of red snails' shells from which hung eight shrimps made of gold.

It was a strange period. There was neither peace nor war. Cortés eventually forced Moctezuma to stay with him. He and Moctezuma played games together and apparently had long talks that Malinche translated, but it wasn't clear whether Moctezuma was a hostage or not. Cortés claimed that he offered to allow Moctezuma to return to his own palace, but Moctezuma refused. If it was true, maybe Moctezuma was worried his own nobles would kill him. Maybe Moctezuma was fascinated by the Spaniards.

Then Cortés got bad news. His old enemy, Velázquez, had sent ships to Mexico under General Pánfilo de Narváez with orders to seize and execute Cortés for sailing off without his permission. Leaving 80 soldiers in Tenochtitlán under the command of Pedro de Alvarado, Cortés marched back to the coast to deal with Narváez. He attacked Narváez at night, something that almost never happened in Spanish warfare. Narváez lost an eye in the battle. Cortés ended up taking 1,000 Spanish prisoners. He offered them two options: to be put to death on the spot or to join him and share the loot that he showed them. Guess which one they chose? All except Narváez, that is, so Cortés threw him into prison where he stayed for almost three years.

When Cortés got back to Tenochtitlán, he found out that Alvarado had led an attack on unarmed Aztecs at a religious festival dance. The Spaniards killed hundreds, leaving their guts spilling out on the temple grounds. This was finally too much for the Aztec elite. They got together and decided that even with Moctezuma kept as a prisoner they would attack the Spaniards. They voted to elect a new emperor, Moctezuma's brother, Cuitlahuac.

Cuitlahuac was not afraid of the Spaniards. When Cortés got back to the city and tried to negotiate peace, Cuitlahuac told his ambassadors to tell the Spaniards there would be no more negotiations. Instead, they would rip the Spaniards' hearts out, cut off their heads and display them in the temple, and chop off their arms and legs and feed them to the animals in the royal zoo.

This did not sound like a good idea to Cortés and his

Sounds to me like negotiations did not go so well.

men. They holed up in the palace and tried to figure out how they were going to escape. Cortés still had his royal hostage, Moctezuma. Moctezuma told Cortés, "I think you all will die." Cortés led the emperor up to the rooftop and commanded him to order his people to go back to their homes. The Aztec warriors cursed Moctezuma for not throwing the Spaniards out earlier. A stone struck Moctezuma in the head. Other arrows hit Moctezuma in the leg and hip. The Spaniards carried him back. Cortés tried to help him, but Moctezuma refused help. Three days later he was dead.

On June 30, 1520, Cortés ordered his men to try to sneak out at night. Some of Cortés's original group were smart enough to travel light, but Narváez's men tried to pack as much gold as they could carry. Many of them fell into the lake and drowned, weighed down by the gold and silver they were stealing. A woman doing laundry in a canal saw them and alerted the Aztec army, which was ready. The Spanish tried to run. Cuitlahuac,

Maybe we can outrun them — I noticed one of them was wearing gold shoes.

the new emperor, ordered his army to kill every Spaniard they could find.

Of the 1,500 Spanish soldiers who were with Cortés, 1,100 were killed. Every single one of the 400 survivors was wounded, including Cortés. Almost all of the more than 10,000 Tlaxcalans were killed. All the cannon was lost and almost all the gold and jewels the Spaniards had tried to steal were gone. With the cries of the dying all around him, Cortés leaned against a cypress tree and cried like a baby.

Exhausted, Cortés got what was left of his men moving. They fought their way back to Tlaxcala, where Cortés and the others licked their wounds and plotted ways to get back to Tenochtitlán and the gold they had left behind. More and more of the Aztecs' enemies came to join the Spaniards.

Meanwhile, it turned out that someone on Narváez's ship had smallpox. Within a month, a smallpox epidemic was raging through Mexico. Aztecs died by the thousands. Cuitlahuac died of smallpox just 28 days after being crowned emperor. A new Aztec emperor was elected, Cuauhtemoc. He was famous for his military cunning and his violent hatred of the Spaniards.

Cortés knew the smallpox epidemic was doing his work for him. After six months in Tlaxcala, he decided it was time to try to attack Tenochtitlán again. He now had more than 1,000 Spanish soldiers who had joined him from Cuba and some 100,000 allies from the surrounding city-states who had joined him and the Tlaxcalans. Cortés and his allies surrounded Tenochtitlán and cut off the city's water supply.

That's not easy to do with a city built in the middle of a lake.

The fighting went on for months. The Aztecs, always good warriors, had figured out how to use the Spaniards' own weapons. They used captured Spanish swords on top of long spears to kill the cavalry horses. They fought by guerrilla warfare, luring the conquistadores into ambushes. When they captured Spanish soldiers alive, they sacrificed them in their temples. Across the lake, Cortés and his men had to watch and listen to the screams of their comrades as they were dragged up the temple steps. Sometimes even horses were dragged up the steps and sacrificed.

At one point during the siege, the Aztecs once again had Cortés trapped. They could have killed the conquistador, but they wanted to capture him alive in order to sacrifice him. That gave one of the Spanish soldiers time to save Cortés by cutting off the hands of the Aztecs who had seized him.

Cortés reportedly told his men that while a single Aztec remained alive, the war would continue. In one skirmish, Cortés killed 800 unarmed women and children looking for food in the streets of the city. Aztec bodies lay dying everywhere. Emperor Cuauhtemoc was captured on August 13, 1520. He begged Cortés to kill him. Cortés refused, and instead hugged the emperor and told him how brave he was. Then Cortés demanded to know where Moctezuma's treasure was hidden.

When Cuauhtemoc wouldn't tell, Cortés had him tortured, but he still wouldn't tell. The mystery of where the bulk of Moctezuma's private hoard of gold, silver, and jewels was hidden has never been solved. Treasure hunters are still searching for it. Still, even without Moctezuma's private fortune, there was plenty of loot for the Spaniards.

I guess this will have to do.

Cortés sent the king of Spain a cannon made completely of melted-down silver. He also sent three treasure ships filled with gold, an emerald as big as a person's palm, and three jaguars. One of the jaguars broke loose on ship and killed two Spaniards and then jumped into the sea. Jaguars are very good swimmers.

Hey, jaguars were sacred to the Aztecs. We don't like to see our people get pushed around.

The End of the Aztec Empire, but Not of the People

Cortés decided to build the capital of "New Spain" on top of the ruins of Tenochtitlán. He forced the Aztecs to tear down their own temples. The great cathedral and central square of present-day Mexico City are made from stones from Aztec temples. The Spaniards burned all but 11 of what must have been thousands of Aztec codices, or books. The Aztec religion was outlawed. Still, unlike the Caribbean islanders, the people survived. They were not *all* killed off by disease or warfare. There were some areas of Mexico that the Spaniards could never quite conquer.

Good evening.

This is Mel Roach reporting live from the once mighty city of Tenochtitlán, and from looks of it, I'm about the only thing that's actually "live" in this place. According to local eye-witnesses, Spanish conquistador Hernán Cortés finally got his hands on something every explorer wants — no, not a taco platter topped with sour cream and guacamole. Gold! The Aztecs fought bravely but soon discovered that if the Spaniards don't get you with their guns and steel swords, then they'd get you with their smallpox. Oh, the horror!

Sadly, the great Aztec emperor Moctezuma also perished in the fighting, but those who knew him assure me Moctezuma will get his revenge.

Reporting live from Tenochtitlán, this is Mel Roach for W-MEL TV. I return you now to the book in progress.

Chapter 7

This Land Belongs to Me, Me, Me!

As the treasures from the Aztecs flowed into Spain, all of a sudden it dawned on everyone in Europe that Columbus hadn't stumbled on a string of a few worthless islands. There was *real* gold and silver in the new land. Now more than ever, other European countries wanted in on the land grab.

Almost daily, the Spaniards sent back ships filled with Aztec gold and silver. They soon added loot from the Incas in Peru, South America.

TIME LINE

1524
Verrazano, sailing for the French, enters New York harbor

1528–1536
Cabeza de Vaca and Esteban wander through Texas

1533
Cortés searches for imaginary land of "California Amazons"

1535
The Iroquois lead Jacques Cartier dow the St. Lawrence Riv

1539
The Zuni kill Esteba de Soto invades Flor Georgia, Alabama, a Mississippi

124

Here we go again.

Pirates cruised the Atlantic Ocean, on the look-out for Spanish ships. English and French pirates became particularly good at stealing the Spaniards' gold.

The King of France, Francis I, decided it was time for the French to get into the "rent-an-explorer" business. Like King Henry VII of England, the French king didn't care about the pope's treaty, especially now that real gold had been found.

Welcome to Rent-an-Explorer. May I help you?

Verrazano Sails In and Out of New York Harbor

In 1523, the French king commissioned Giovanni da Verrazano, a sea captain from Florence, Italy, to sail for France. On March 1, 1524, Verrazano sighted land near what is today Cape Fear, North Carolina. Verrazano kept going north.

On April 17, 1524, Verrazano sailed into

He gets eaten, but not by New Yorkers.

what he called one of the finest harbors in the world, "a very agreeable place between two small hills." One of the hills is on what is now Staten Island and the other is in Brooklyn, New York. Verrazano also has the distinction of being the first European explorer to actually be eaten by cannibals. For the record, that hap-

pened on an island off South America, not in
New York City.

Chief Donnacona, Jacques Cartier, and the Naming of Canada

Ten years later, in 1534, the king of France
commissioned another explorer, Jacques Cartier,
who made it across the Atlantic Ocean in just 20
days. He arrived on the east coast of Newfoundland. He then sailed into the mouth of the
St. Lawrence River, near what is now Quebec,
Canada. Cartier was met by a Huron leader
named Donnacona. Cartier asked Donnacona
what they called the place. Donnacona answered
"kanata," most likely meaning the small settle-
ment that he lived in. The Huron never gave a
region a general name. They only named towns
and natural features, such as rivers or mountains. However, "Kanada" or "Cannata" was an
easy word for the French to say. Cartier began to
call the entire area "Kanada," and that's how
Canada got its name.

Donnacona and his sons led Cartier down
the St. Lawrence River; because of its currents,
the river is extremely tricky to navigate. The
group got as far as what is now Montreal when
the French sailors got sick with scurvy, which
comes from not eating enough vitamin C. The
Iroquois taught the French sailors how to cure

their illness by brewing a tea made from the bark of pine trees.

The Itch to Get Rich: De Soto Goes to Florida

Meanwhile, the Spaniards were taking advantage of their head start in what was now called the New World. Among them was one Hernando de Soto.

De Soto was born around 1500. His dad was a poor Spanish squire. As a kid, he heard fabulous stories about the adventures of his neighbor Balboa, who had traveled to the West Indies. De Soto wanted to go to the New World, too. He did, learning a thing or two from conquistadores like Cortés and Pizarro. Although de Soto got rich quickly after plundering Nicaragua and Peru, he yearned for still more success and glory. He wanted to find an empire in Florida as magnificent as

the Inca empire in Peru. The rest, as they say, is history.

De Soto did not travel light. In 1538, he invaded Florida with more than 600 men, a mix of officers, soldiers, and slaves. Some of the slaves were Africans; others were the surviving Arawaks. He also shipped along 240 mules and packhorses, 13 pigs that he hoped would be a kind of walking supply of bacon for his troops, 3,800 bushels of maize, a pack of 100 bloodhounds and wolfhounds all trained to attack, a supply of neck chains for capturing new slaves, and an anvil (to make more chains).

De Soto and his men landed near what is now Fort Myers, Florida. It was the home of the Timucua, who were part of the Mississippian cultures. The Timucua were good fighters and started attacking the Spaniards immediately. When they couldn't completely defeat the Spaniards, they disappeared into the forests to get ready to fight again. De Soto had brought all those supplies but not enough men to carry them, thinking that he could pick up slaves along the way. Surprise! It wasn't as easy to enslave the people of the Southeast as he had thought.

De Soto marched north, spending three months near Georgia and South Carolina. In Georgia, he encountered the princess of Talomecco, who protected her queen by giving de Soto pearls and then escaping. The pearls only whetted de Soto's appetite for finding gold and precious stones.

Speaking of appetites, are we going to start talking about food again soon? I'm starving!

De Soto and his army crossed the Appalachian Mountains and entered the kingdom of the Coosa and the Cherokee in what is now Georgia, Alabama, and Tennessee. De Soto and the Spaniards were amazed by the Coosas' rich agricultural fields and their great temple mounds. They came to the village of Tuscaloosa and met a leader who was carried on a litter, accompanied by 1,000 men. When de Soto demanded that the

Tuscaloosa carry his supplies for him, the ruler replied that they served no one but themselves. De Soto had him put in chains. The chief, who also went by the name Tuscaloosa, sent a message ahead, warning the other Coosa tribes to gather for war against

You're just like the rest of the explorers: lazy and mean.

the Spanish in the town of Mabilla, now Mobile, Alabama.

The Battle of Mabilla

When de Soto got to Mabilla, he found a town fortified against attack. He read out the Requirement. The Coosa warriors poured out of the town to do battle. Several times it looked as if the Coosas had won. But late in the day, some of the Spanish soldiers got close enough to the town to burn the Coosas' wooden huts. In less than an hour, the village was destroyed.

Two thousand Coosas lay dead. The Spaniards had only 20 dead and 148 wounded, but they had lost all their supplies.

After the battle of Mabilla, de Soto pushed his army through Alabama. He then went

Alabama Museum of Natural History, University of Alabama, Tuscaloosa, Alabama Besides having many exhibits about the Coosa people, the museum runs field trips to nearby Moundville Archaeological Park, which is 13 miles away. This was probably where de Soto met the Tuscaloosa.

through what is now the state of Mississippi. On May 21, 1541, de Soto came to a wide river that he named the Río del Espíritu Santo (River of the Holy Ghost), which we call the Mississippi River. Our word comes from two Natchez words: *michi* meaning big and *sippi* meaning water.

> What can I say? I like to be carried.

De Soto and his ragtag army crossed the Mississippi River into what is now Arkansas. He entered the nation of the Natchez. He met Quigaltam, the Great Leader of the Natchez, who was carried on a litter so that his feet would never touch the ground.

Shortly after meeting the Natchez, de Soto came down with a fever. On May 21, 1542, exactly a year after he had reached the Mississippi River, he died. The few Spaniards who survived made it back to Cuba, cursing the fact that they had ever made the trip. Unfortunately, one of the men traveling with de Soto was infected with smallpox. Within a short while, many women, men, and children would be dead throughout the Southeast.

The Search for the Seven Cities of Gold

Pánfilo de Narváez, the man who had lost an eye fighting Cortés, also wanted to find the legendary cities of gold and outdo his old enemy, Cortés. When Cortés finally let him out of prison in 1523, he went back to Spain with a silk eye patch worn over his eye. He was positive he could

This is not going to be easy with just one eye.

find a land even richer than the Aztec empire. He already knew where he wanted to find it — in Florida.

In 1528, Narváez sailed from Spain with seven ships and 600 men and a couple of women. Among the men on that trip were Álvar Núñez

Cabeza de Vaca, whose last name means head of a cow, and Esteban, a black slave from Morocco who belonged to a Spaniard named Andrés Dorantes. Esteban was a big man with a bull neck and a strong body. He had to be strong. He was about to survive eight years of wandering from Florida to Texas. He would soon become famous for his colorful headgear and outfits.

Narváez landed near what is now Tampa Bay, Florida, and almost immediately got lost. He met powerful warriors, the Apalachen, near the Florida-Georgia border. The Apalachen used a particularly strong bow, more powerful than the European crossbow. It was as thick as a man's wrist and very accurate. Unlike the Aztecs, the Apalachen did not fight in open battalions. They hid in the trees and in swamps, breathing through reeds. Then they'd sneak up behind the Spaniards and attack from the rear. In 1776, 250 years later, the rebellious Americans would use the same tactics against the English. Nearly 200

Does anybody else feel like we're being watched?

years after that, the Vietnamese would use those same tactics against the Americans, proving that in history, everything old is new again.

Does anybody else remember where we parked?

Narváez and his survivors retreated from the Apalachen, losing more men each day. When the Spaniards finally got back to the sea, they couldn't find their boats. They made rafts and floated out to sea. Narváez died at sea. Cabeza de Vaca and Esteban drifted on separate rafts to Texas. The 84 men with Cabeza de Vaca landed on what is now Galveston Island, off the coast of Texas. They were half starving, crazed with thirst, and they had landed on one of the most barren islands in North America. The exact name of the people who greeted Cabeza de Vaca on Galveston has been lost to history. However, despite the fact that they had little to eat themselves, those North Americans took pity on the

Spaniards and helped them, even bursting into tears at the sight of the Spaniards' misery.

Cabeza de Vaca was impressed with their kindness toward one another. "Of all the people in the world, they are those who most love their children and treat them best." By winter, the Spaniards, now down to only 15 in number, were put to work digging for plants.

In the spring Cabeza de Vaca became sick. His Spanish comrades took off for what they hoped was Mexico. They were never heard from again. Cabeza de Vaca was left to die somewhere on the mainland of Texas near the Gulf of Mexico. But he didn't die. He became a kind of peddler. He learned a sign language that the North Americans used among themselves. They were awful years for him, years of loneliness and near starvation, during which he thought he was going mad.

Esteban: A Gift for Gab

Esteban, being an African from the western coast of Morocco, already spoke Spanish and Arabic. Cabeza de Vaca noted that in their journeys, the people they ran into spoke different languages and that Esteban was the most skilled at learning the languages of the natives of Texas. Cabeza de Vaca wrote that Esteban was "constantly in conversation, finding out about routes, towns, and other matters we wished to know." Esteban also became a favorite of the women he met.

In 1532, de Vaca came to a village in Texas. To his shock, he found Esteban, his owner, Dorantes, and another Spaniard named Castillo still alive. They hugged one another and wept. For the next six years, the four walked more than 1,000 miles through Texas, trying to find their way back to Mexico. They were often guided by nomadic, poor North Americans, perhaps Anasazi refugees, fleeing from the Apache and Zuni of New Mexico and Arizona.

Esteban and Cabeza de Vaca earned reputations as healers. Their healing techniques consisted of imitating tribal medicine, blowing on the injured parts of people's bodies, and chanting Catholic prayers. The men's reputation as healers spread, and as they traveled through the Southwest, they were given gifts and welcomed by the tribes they met. Esteban was considered a very powerful healer and was given a sacred rattle made of a gourd. It had one red feather, one white feather, and a little string of bells. He would use the rattle to "chase" the sickness out of the person who was ill.

At some point, the three surviving Spaniards and Esteban crossed the Rio Grande into what is now the Big Bend country of Texas. They followed the Rio Grande to the site of present-day El Paso, Texas. There, they were given gifts of five arrowheads made of beautifully cut emeralds. It was the first hint of wealth they had found. It was enough to convince them that they must be near the legendary seven cities of gold.

I think they were just delirious from walking around so much.

Esteban, Cabeza de Vaca, Dorantes, and Castillo were finally rescued nearly eight years after their shipwreck. When they arrived back in Mexico City it was as if they had returned from the dead. They spread the word that the seven cities of gold were just north of "New Spain." Everyone wanted to hear their stories, especially the ones about those golden cities, the ones with the emeralds.

In the Texas wilderness, Esteban had been a free man. He told the new governor of Mexico that he would be glad to lead the Spaniards back to the seven cities of gold. The Spaniards would not let a black man actually lead, even though he was the only one who knew where they were going. The new governor bought Esteban from Dorantes and gave him to a clergyman named Fray Marcos, who was anxious to see the seven cities of gold. They took off from Mexico City.

Esteban Overestimates

On the journey north, Esteban wore a bright-colored robe and a hat with rare feathers. He carried his sacred rattle with him. He didn't stay with Fray Marcos long. As soon as they crossed the Rio Grande, Esteban traveled up ahead with his two greyhound dogs at his side. As he went through villages, he'd shake his rattle and ask for women. And usually he got them.

Finally, he reached the Zuni city of Hawikuh near the Arizona-New Mexico border. When he

That never works for me! Never!

got near the city, he sent his rattle ahead as usual. This was a big mistake! Esteban apparently had added some Spanish bells to his rattles. The Zunis already hated the Spaniards for raiding the Pueblo tribes for slaves. In a great rage, the Zuni leader flung the rattle to the ground and told Esteban to leave the city. Esteban laughed at the Zuni leader. Not only that, he demanded turquoise and women — another bad move.

The elders put Esteban in a hut outside the village and deliberated for three days about what to do with him. The Zuni decided to kill him, some say with arrows, others say by cutting his body into little pieces.

Either way, the end result was the same.

Myths of History

Some think that Esteban only pretended to be dead in order to escape slavery, but since nobody ever heard from him again, it's pretty likely that he did end up very dead.

Coronado on the March

I saw a huge city of gold . . . then I caught a fish this big.

Fray Marcos returned to Mexico City, apparently infected with Esteban's need to exaggerate. Fray Marcos told the governor and everyone who would listen that he had seen a city bigger than the great golden Aztec city of Tenochtitlán.

The governor of New Spain gave Francisco Vásquez de Coronado the job of leading an army up north and finding Fray Marcos's great golden cities. Coronado's army was the most impressive one ever assembled for exploration of the New World. It cost the equivalent of two million dollars in today's U.S. money to assemble.

As Coronado and his army marched out of Mexico City, they must have looked spectacular. They weren't going to look so good when they came back. On the way, horses died, and the soldiers were starving. If it hadn't been for their North American guides, they wouldn't have gotten very far. In the Gila Mountains of what is now Arizona, the North Americans showed the starving soldiers how to make pine nut cakes out of water and ground pine nuts.

Sounds like a gourmet meal to me.

What to Pack to Conquer a Legendary Kingdom

- 230 cavalry, 32 infantry, four friars, one surgeon
- 1,000 Mexicans and their families, 1,000 horses, at least three Spanish wives
- thousands of cattle, sheep, goats, and pigs, for barbecues
- a snazzy wardrobe (Coronado wore a helmet with beautiful plumes and full armor with gold overlay)
- Fray Marcos, the friar who claimed that he'd actually seen one of the cities of gold

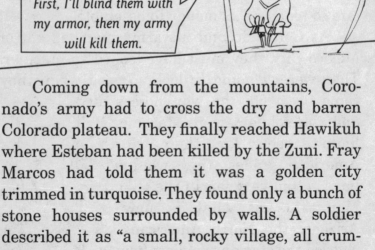

First, I'll blind them with my armor, then my army will kill them.

Coming down from the mountains, Coronado's army had to cross the dry and barren Colorado plateau. They finally reached Hawikuh where Esteban had been killed by the Zuni. Fray Marcos had told them it was a golden city trimmed in turquoise. They found only a bunch of stone houses surrounded by walls. A soldier described it as "a small, rocky village, all crumpled up."

I guess they redecorated.

The soldiers cursed Fray Marcos. One soldier wrote, "Such were the curses hurled at him that I prayed God might protect him." Coronado couldn't stand the sight of him and sent him back to Mexico City in disgrace. He went back to his monastery, and nobody knows what happened to him after that.

Here we go again!

The Zuni elders were no more happy to see Coronado than they had been to see Esteban. They formed a line of cornmeal on the ground and told Coronado he could go no farther. Coronado read the Requirement. The Zuni attacked.

Coronado as Fashion Victim

The battle lasted only about an hour and a half. The only major Spanish injury was to Coronado. Decked out in his shiny armor, he made a good target for the Zuni. Unable to pierce his armor with arrows, they pelted him with rocks and knocked him out. He probably would have died if his soldiers hadn't dragged his body away. Coronado's army still managed to take the city and the surrounding pueblos. They actually learned to admire the Pueblo way of life. One soldier wrote, "The holy men tell them how to live, and I believe they are given certain commandments for them to keep, for there is no drunkenness among them . . . nor sacrifices. They are usually at work."

Coronado, recovering from his wounds, soon realized there was no gold to be found in the immediate vicinity. He sent his men in all directions looking for the golden cities. One of his men, Pedro de Castañeda, came across the Grand Canyon. Today, it is considered one of the wonders of the world. To the Spaniards, it was a "useless piece of country." Coronado's men tried to climb down the Grand Canyon and failed.

Zuni Pueblo and Hawikuh The Zuni Pueblo is about 30 miles southwest of Gallup, New Mexico. The Zuni people still live on this site. They have created a museum that shows Zuni history and culture.

The Tigua Rebellion in New Mexico

Coronado crossed the Rio Grande and ended up at the home of the Tigua, a group of Pueblo people who had lived in this valley of New Mexico for centuries. At first they greeted the Spaniards warmly. Then Coronado ordered the Tigua people to get out of the houses that they had built and get to work giving the Spaniards all the food that they had.

This seemed like a horrible idea to the Tigua. In 1541, they rebelled. There were many fierce battles; as soon as the Spaniards put down one town, another town would attack. In one battle, both sides made signs of peace, but when the Tigua went to negotiate, Coronado had 200 of them burned at the stake.

Other Tigua continued to fight back. The fighting went on all winter. The Tigua people fled rather than be enslaved by Coronado. When the spring finally came, Coronado left.

Buffalo Buffet

I WENT ALL THE WAY TO KANSAS AND ALL I GOT WAS THIS LOUSY T-SHIRT

Coronado and his men crossed the Great Plains and saw seas of buffalo. The Spaniards wrote that they didn't know how to describe the number of buffalo except to say that it was like the fish in the sea. The Spaniards hunted the buffalo on horseback, and very soon the Lakota and other North Americans of the Great Plains would use captured Spanish horses to hunt buffalo themselves.

Coronado and his men got as far as Kansas, where they found people living in grass huts. They didn't find any cities of gold. Coronado began his slow retreat. By now, many of his men were dead. He came back to Mexico City empty-handed.

California Girls—400 Years Before the Beach Boys

The first Europeans to explore the beaches of California were looking for girls. It's also a fact that books can change history. In 1510, Garci de Montalva wrote a book called *Les sergas de Esplandían*. It is the story of a virtuous Spanish cavalier who visits the New World and finds an island called "California, very near Paradise, which was ruled by Queen Calafia and her court of powerful women, their arms all of gold."

This is the first known use of the word "California," a word that the writer seems to have made up. The legend of Amazon women had fascinated many of the Spanish explorers, including Amerigo Vespucci and Columbus. Hernán Cortés, apparently having read *Les sergas de Esplandían* and having heard tall tales from a sea captain about an island full of women, wanted to find those "California Amazons."

In 1535, Cortés sailed north from Mexico to what is now the Mexican state of Baja California. He stayed there for almost a year and took possession of it for Spain. Then he realized that his rivals in Mexico City were getting him kicked out as governor there, and he hurried back.

These explorers will believe anything! Hey, buddy, wanna buy a bridge?

I think we should call this land California. What does that mean? I don't know, but it sure sounds nice, doesn't it?

The idea of finding California, the island of women, still fascinated many Spaniards. In 1541, another Spaniard, Francisco de Polanos, sailed north, again to Baja. Polanos was the first to use the word "California" for the new land, and it is thought that he called it that because of Montalva's novel.

North America's First Journalist

Juan Rodríguez was one of the Spaniards who had landed in Mexico in 1520 with Narváez's army to arrest Cortés. He ended up staying and becoming rich. By the 1540s, Rodríguez had settled down on the western coast near Guatemala and started a shipbuilding business. When an earthquake hit the area in 1541, he wrote about it in a pamphlet. It has been called the beginning of journalism in America. But that's not why Juan Rodríguez is famous. He became famous for being the first Spaniard to sail up the coastline of California.

Juan Rodríguez did not think of himself as a

journalist. Rich as he was, like almost all the early Spaniards, he wanted more. In 1542, he set sail for California with supplies for two years. His men called him Cabrillo, which means "little goat," and the name stuck. On September 28, 1542, he sailed into a harbor that he called San Miguel. The people who lived there were the Diegue-os. It was a heavily populated area with perhaps has many as 20,000 people living around the bay. Today, the city is called San Diego after its original inhabitants.

Cabrillo sailed north from San Diego. At first, people such as the Chumash and Pomo who lived along the California coast were glad to trade. They liked the Spaniards' metal tools and their cloth. Cabrillo was impressed by how much food

Cabrillo National Monument, San Diego, has a small museum about Juan Rodríguez Cabrillo and a wonderful view of the harbor, which is a great place to see the winter gray whale migration. The annual Cabrillo Festival, held every September 28, includes a reenactment of the Spaniards' arrival.

the California Americans had to trade and how well they lived. He continued sailing north to what is now Point Reyes, outside San Francisco. He and his sailors hated the place. It was foggy and cold. They couldn't wait to turn around. They did *not* leave their hearts in San Francisco.

The coldest winter I ever spent was a summer in San Francisco.

Cabrillo sailed south and ended up spending the winter in what is now Santa Barbara, California. The Chumash and Pomo were not happy to see them again. The Spanish were always demanding food and refusing to trade much for it. On Christmas Eve 1542, Cabrillo tried to get some fresh water from land. His men were attacked. When Cabrillo jumped out of the boat, he turned out *not* to be as nimble as a little goat. He broke his leg on the rocky coast — something surfers still are in danger of doing today. His leg became infected and he died. Cabrillo's men sailed north, running into huge winter storms. They may have pushed as far north as Oregon. They turned around and arrived back in Mexico on April 14, 1543, their ships battered and leaking. The sailors reported that they hadn't found much gold or much of anything, and certainly no island of Amazonian women.

For Better or Worse

By the 1540s, ships were sailing back and forth from Europe to North America in just a few weeks. Explorers, conquerors, guys who got

That would have to wait until the United States women's soccer team won the World Cup in 1999. Many of those players were California Amazons.

shipwrecked and wandered around and got lost, it doesn't matter what they're called. The two worlds were now bound together, for better or worse, just like a marriage.

The Vikings came and left after a few years. The Europeans who came after Columbus were *not* going to leave. Some had children with the people who were already here. Others came with women from Europe and started families. Soon, there would be whole new generations who couldn't say they were really natives of England, Spain, France, or Africa. They were people who were born in the New World.

After the worlds collided, the fate of the Americas and the fate of the rest of the world got mixed up together. Food changed for everybody. Cows, pigs, sheep, chickens, onions, barley, oats, lettuces, peaches, pears, and watermelon all came to North America, brought over by the Europeans. In Europe, taste in foods changed even more. It didn't take long for European farmers to begin planting corn, tomatoes, and especially potatoes. Potatoes became one of Europe's most important crops.

I sure hope all this stuff tastes good with corn.

The people who had been living in North America for tens of thousands of years did like some of the things that the Europeans brought. It was much easier to chase a bison on horseback than on foot, and they were happy to have iron and steel tools. The Europeans were thrilled with all the silver and gold that they found or *took*, especially in Mexico. They also liked many

I can't believe we didn't steal this idea years ago!

of the inventions that they found. Soon, almost all European sailors were using Arawak hammocks to sleep in when they sailed. Europeans learned how to cure many diseases, such as scurvy, which had made them sick for hundreds of generations.

But the continent and its original people changed everyone who came — and after the year 1540, many more Europeans were coming. These colonists were supposed to be loyal to the kings and queens they had left behind, but some of these new colonials would get mighty cranky. They would come to think of themselves as a new people; they would think of themselves as Americans. In fact, some, you might say, were even revolting, but that's another Horrible History. . . .

Well, everyone,

that's the story of the European explorers, and what a bunch they were! From the Ericksson family to Christopher Columbus to Hernán Cortés, they came to the New World and demanded things that didn't belong to them. Sounds like a bully I once had to deal with in school. How was I supposed to know all I had to do was give him piles of gold and he would stop taking my lunch money?

There's no denying that these explorers were a brave lot to sail off on such incredible voyages in the first place, but I get the feeling they might not have gotten in so many fights if they just tried to be nicer wherever they landed.

Yep, gold does funny things to people. There are those who will risk their lives (and lots of others' lives) and go for the gold! Personally, I don't care for it much. Gold clashes with my skin tone, and it tastes horrible!

In our next book, we'll learn about a group of people who didn't care as much about gold as they did about their freedom. Don't get me wrong, they loved gold. It's just that they

realized some things don't have to glitter to be valuable.

Hope I see you again soon!

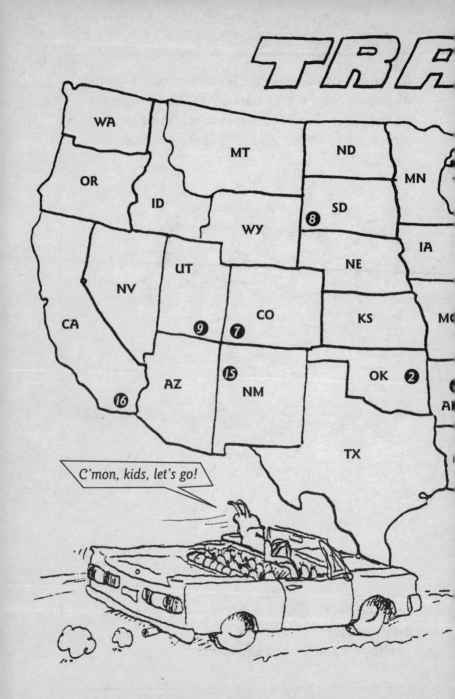

1a.-1b. Natchez Trace Parkway, Natchez, Mississippi, to Nashville, Tennessee, p. 37

2. Spiro Mounds State Archaeological Site, Spiro, Oklahoma, p. 37

3. Etowah Mounds Historic Site, Georgia, p. 37

4. Moundville Archeological Park, Alabama, p. 37

5. Cahokia Mound State Historical Site, Illinois, p. 37

6. Toltec Mounds Archaeological State Park, Arkansas, p. 37

7. Outdoor museum, Mesa Verde National Park, Colorado, p. 39

8. Sioux Indian Museum, Rapid City, South Dakota, p.39

9. Monument Valley Navajo Tribal Park, Utah, p. 39

10. Tantaquidegeon Lodge Museum and Foxboro Museum, Connecticut, p. 39

11. Mashantucket Pequot Museum, Connecticut, p. 39

12. Pocono Indian Museum, Bushkill, Pennsylvania, p. 39

13. Historical Museum of Southern Florida, Miami, Florida, p.100

14. Alabama Museum of Natural History, University of Alabama, Tuscaloosa, Alabama, p. 132

15. Zuni Pueblo and Hawikuh, New Mexico, p. 144

16. Cabrillo National Monument, San Diego, California, p. 149

Index